ARTIST'S WORKSHOP

OILS LANDSCAPE

Brian and Ursula Bagnall • Astrid Hille

WALTER FOSTER PUBLISHING, INC.
Laguna Hills, California

Published by Walter Foster Publishing, Inc.,
23062 La Cadena Drive, Laguna Hills, CA 92653.

Produced by Joshua Morris Publishing, Inc.

Original German title: *Ölmalerei—Landschaften: Berge, Felder, Wiesen.*
Cover painting by Brian Bagnall.
Printed in Hong Kong.

ISBN: 1-56010-184-9
10 9 8 7 6 5 4 3 2 1

Contents

About This Book

Many people feel that oils are the only type of painting that truly deserves to be called art. Because of this, oils tend to intimidate would-be painters, and many hobbyists never even give this medium a try. Everyone knows that the world's most famous artists painted in oils, and students in art history classes are perpetually confronted with the oil paintings of the inimitable great masters. Even in the case of more modern painting styles like surrealism, oil painting seems to be something that is difficult to learn—something almost unattainable.

This book will help you learn that oil is actually a very patient medium that permits changes and allows you to think things over and rework your composition. At the same time, oil painting requires patience and planning. Although it's difficult to achieve quick, effective results, there are few surprises like the spontaneous mixtures that occur in watercolors. A picture has to be carefully planned and thought out—a way of working that can be very interesting and exciting, and one that allows you to make corrections and improvements.

This book will teach you the basic techniques of oil painting and help you develop your own style. It will also give you the inspiration and confidence to experiment with more unusual ways of working with the medium.

You'll have the opportunity to "look over the shoulder" of four different artists as they show you—step by step—their own personal techniques and preferences for working in oils. In addition, they'll divulge a few of their favorite tricks and provide you with inspiration for finding your own motifs and transferring them to paint. The main concern of this book, however, is to convey to you the joy of oil painting. Have fun!

Ursula Bagnall

Ursula Bagnall is the partner of Brian Bagnall—art director for the Artist's Workshop series—and she is responsible for text and layout. She brings the artists' outlooks, explanations, and paintings together and creates a useful and easy-to-use learning tool.

Ursula was born in 1945 and completed her training in graphic design at the Akademie für Graphisches Gewerbe in Munich. Afterward, she worked with Otl Aicher for the 1972 Olympics and later took a five-year teaching position at an American school in Amsterdam. In addition to freelance work for the Bavarian television station in Germany, she has worked since 1973 as a freelance graphic artist and author. She and her husband have written many books together, among them several art instruction books for children and adults.

Astrid Hille

Astrid Hille is the editor of the Artist's Workshop series and works closely with Bagnall Studios. She was born in 1955 in Hamburg, Germany, where she completed training as a technical illustrator at the Fachhochschule für Kunst und Gestaltung. She later went on to study illustration and painting. After her studies, she worked as an illustrator, painter, and art teacher in adult education. She completed a second degree in multimedia education and has been a proofreader of art books and children's books since 1985.

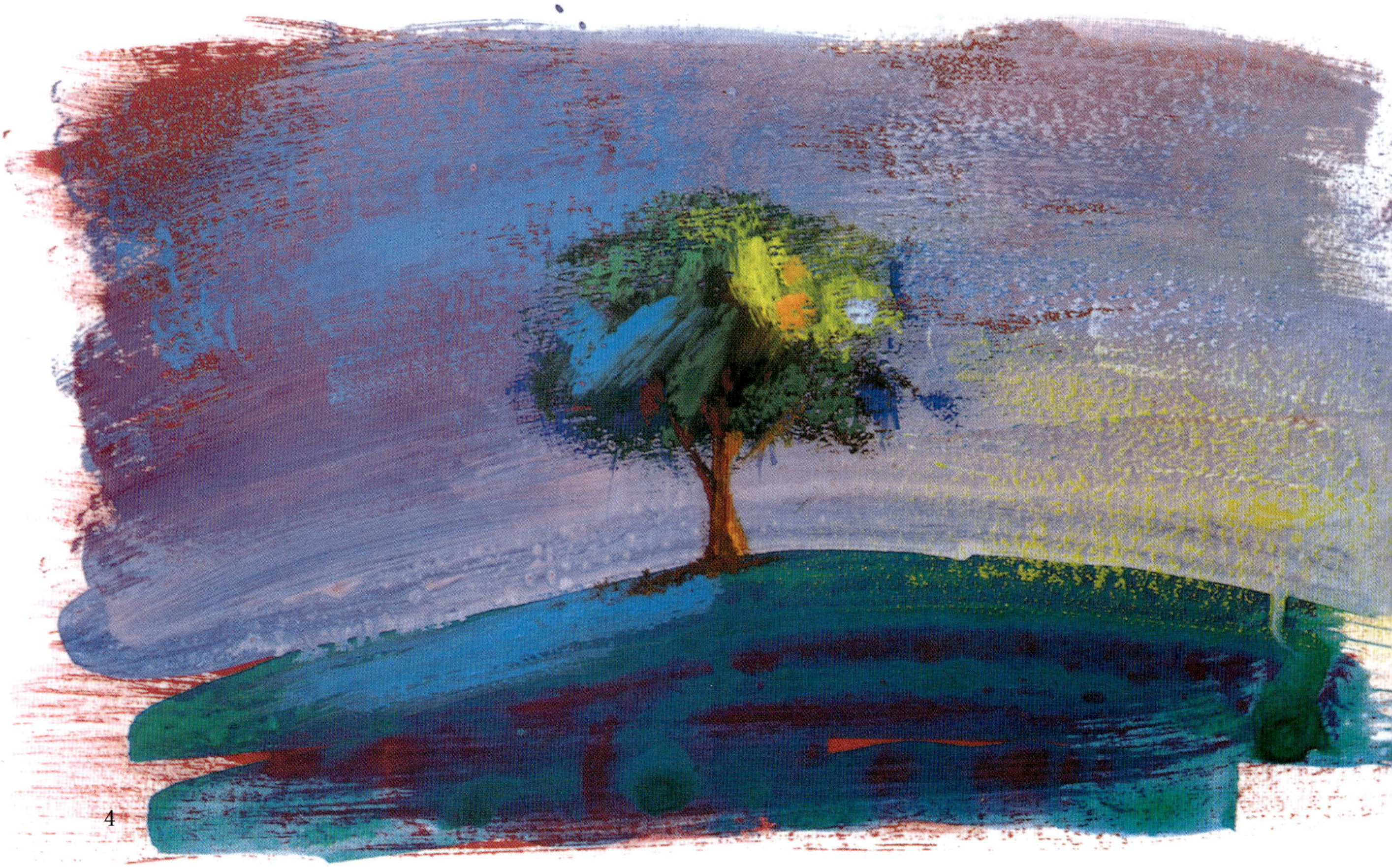

Brian Bagnall

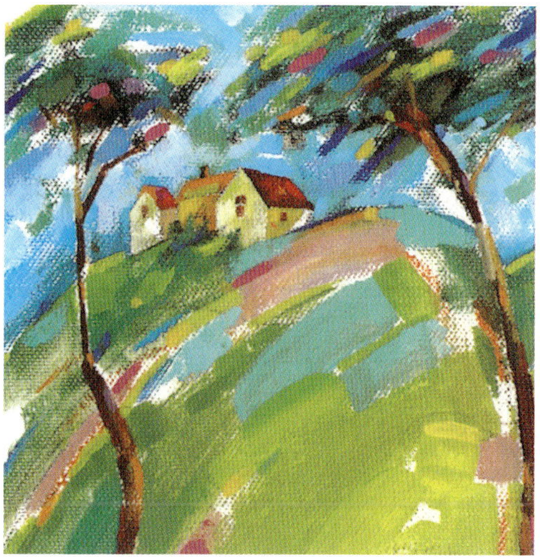

Brian Bagnall will show you how to paint a simple landscape.

Brian was born in 1943 in Wakefield, England. He studied painting and etching and completed his National Diploma with honors. He then moved to Amsterdam where, in addition to teaching, he worked for numerous publishing houses and advertising agencies.

Since 1970 he has lived in Munich, where he and his wife opened Bagnall Studios. Brian was also active for many years as a professor in Darmstadt, Germany. He has written a number of books, and his work has been exhibited all over Europe and Korea.

Edeltraut Klapproth

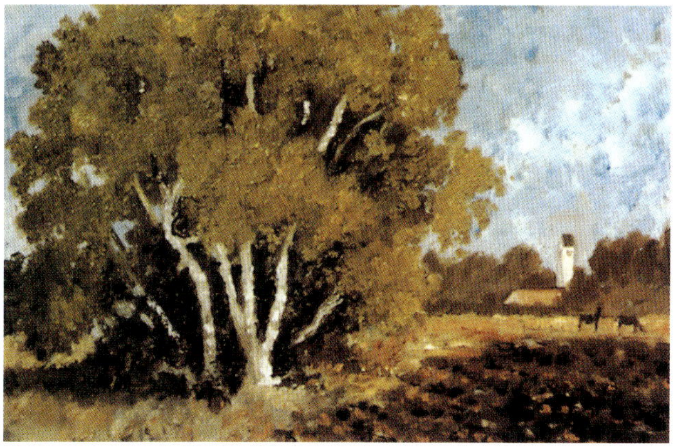

Take Edeltraut Klapproth up on her invitation to walk through the autumn woods and learn about painting nature.

She grew up in the city of Dachau, home to numerous painters. While she was in Munich in the 1920s, she took lessons from some well-known painters of the day. Her artistic endeavors were interrupted by marriage and World War II, however, and she was not able to pick them up again until her children were older. Edeltraut Klapproth has enjoyed success since her first exhibit. She displays her work at least twice a year, without regard for contemporary trends. She never paints anything sad—she says there's already enough sadness in the world.

Christine Meder

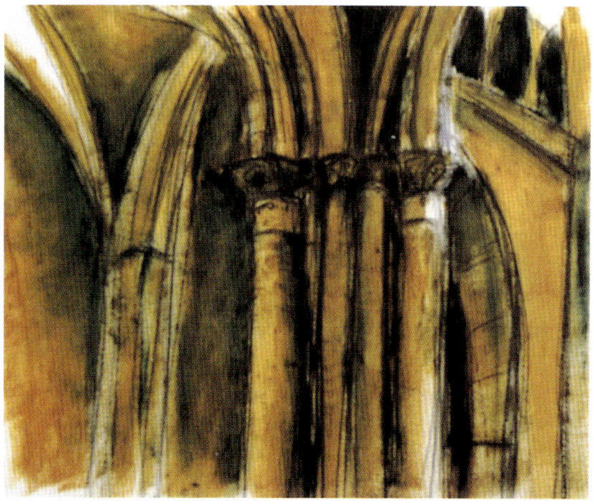

Christine Meder will lead you through a landscape of rooftops.

Born in Erlangen, Germany, in 1961, the artist studied simultaneously at the Akademie für Bildende Künste and the Fachhochschule Kommunkationsdesign in Munich. She works for advertising agencies and the Bavarian television station, where she creates computer graphics and computer animation—quite a contrast to landscape painting! But she paints in her studio when time permits. She says even the most extraordinary experiences at the computer could never replace the smell and feel of oil paints.

Uwe Neuhaus

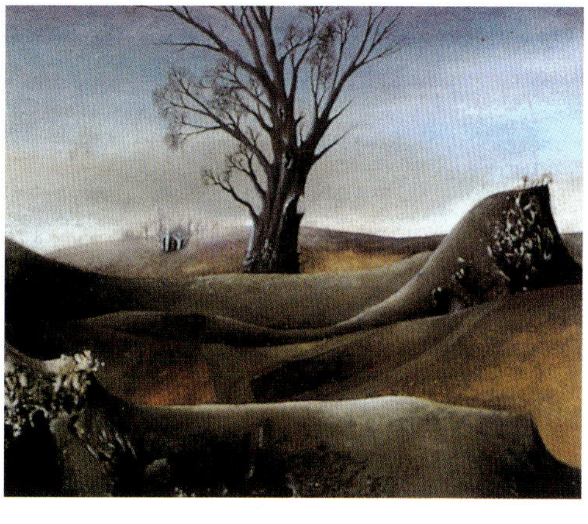

Uwe Neuhaus will paint a beach motif to give you an introduction to surrealism.

Uwe was born in 1942 in Mittenwald, Germany, and studied graphic design and painting in Munich. In 1966 he opened a small gallery in Munich and enjoyed much success with his outlandish and unconventional paintings. He has taken part in numerous solo and group exhibitions in Germany, Italy, and Switzerland. The son of an actor, Mr. Neuhaus holds annual exhibits in his farmhouse in the Allgäu region of Germany. These exhibits, which combine satire and cabaret, enjoy widespread popularity.

Landscapes in Oils—Yesterday and Today

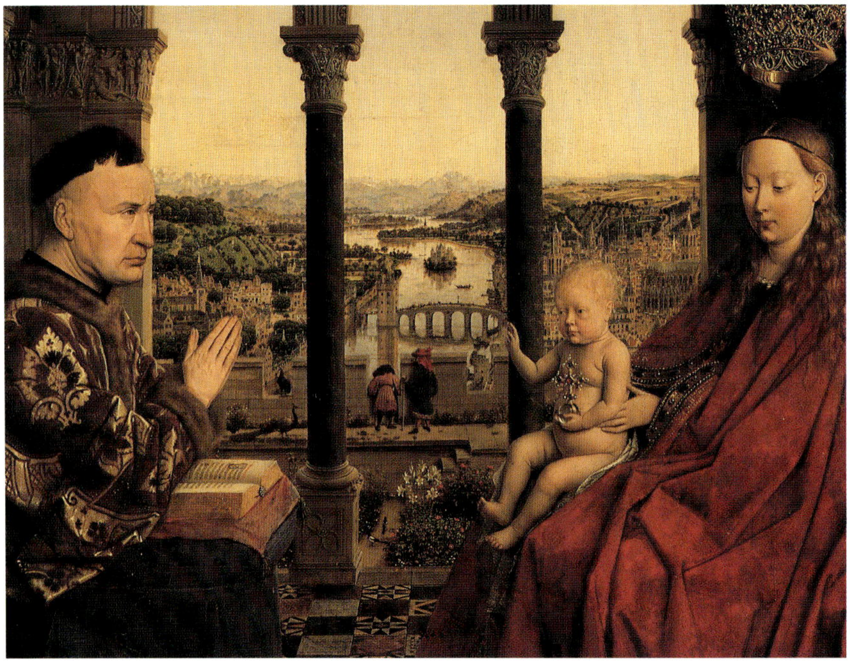

Jan van Eyck, *Madonna with Chancellor Rolin*

Landscape painting, which today is one of the best-known types of painting, was virtually unknown to artists prior to the Renaissance. Of course, individual nature motifs were common, but landscape elements served merely decorative functions within the larger context of the composition. The lack of knowledge about drawing perspective and modeling depth perpetuated the subordinate role of landscape elements. During the symbol-laden Middle Ages, individual objects in nature gained allegorical significance.

With the advent of the Early Renaissance, knowledge about perspective began to increase significantly, and the discovery of one-point perspective in the fifteenth century was of decisive importance. Artists such as Albrecht Dürer (1471–1528) and Leonardo da Vinci (1452–1519) concentrated both on the scientific and artistic aspects of landscape painting. They painted the first "figureless" landscapes, creating a new way of looking at space. Consequently, landscape paintings became more realistic. This new view also corresponded to Jan van Eyck's (1395–1441) objective of painting things the way they actually appear. He left behind a legacy of painting a particular landscape repertoire: A hilly landscape with a city and a river providing the backdrop for a religious motif.

For many years, Jan van Eyck was considered the founder of modern oil painting, but pure oil painting actually didn't come into its own right until the sixteenth century. At first, artists worked with oil-based tempera paints made from resins. Van Eyck began to bind his earth pigments with linseed oil and a kind of turpentine, which allowed his paints to dry more slowly. Still, van Eyck's works cannot be considered pure oil paintings. Like his predecessors, he used a combination of different media, but his contributions certainly constituted a huge step forward in oil painting.

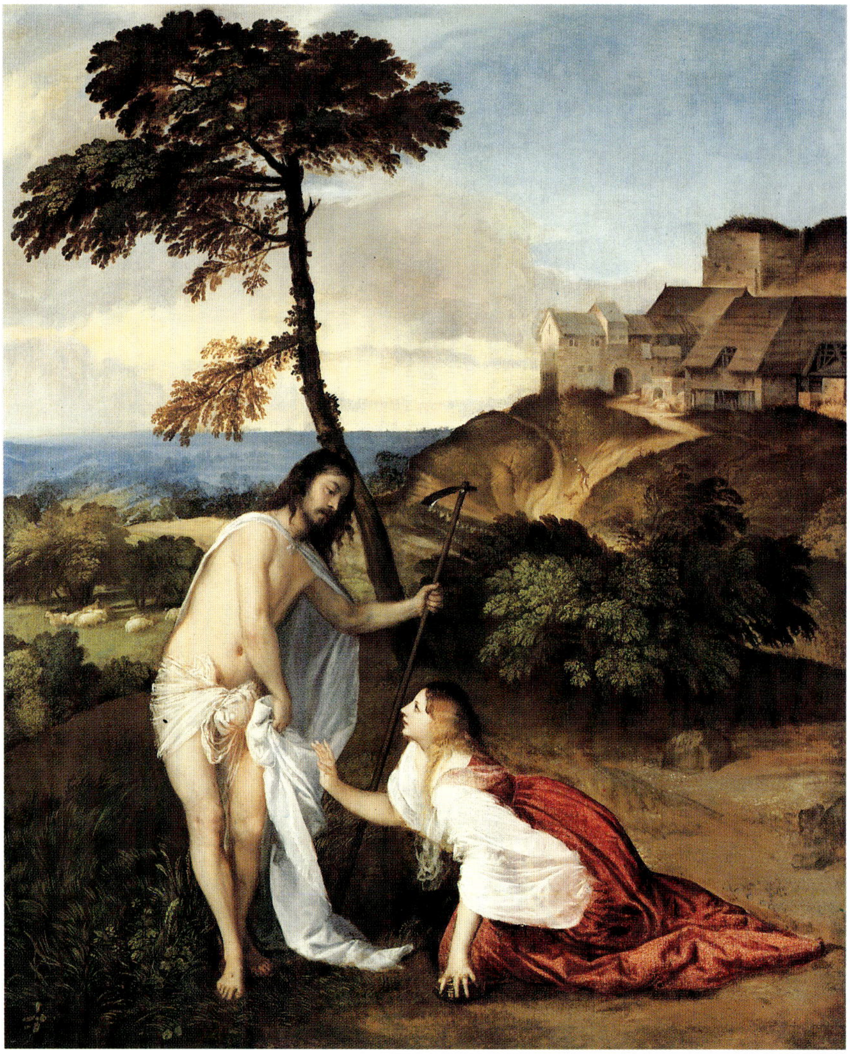

Titian, *Christ Appearing to the Magdalen*

After the seventeenth century, landscape painting became a separate genre. Thematic differences among the types of landscapes—such as seascapes and forests—developed quickly. Landscapes gained depth and became more expressive. Rembrandt, the master of contrast, was able to create deeply dramatic moods in his landscapes. He worked with thick paints, similar in consistency to the oils we know today. In order to create texture in his paintings, Rembrandt would scratch and scrape the paint with the tip of his brush—quite unconventional at the time.

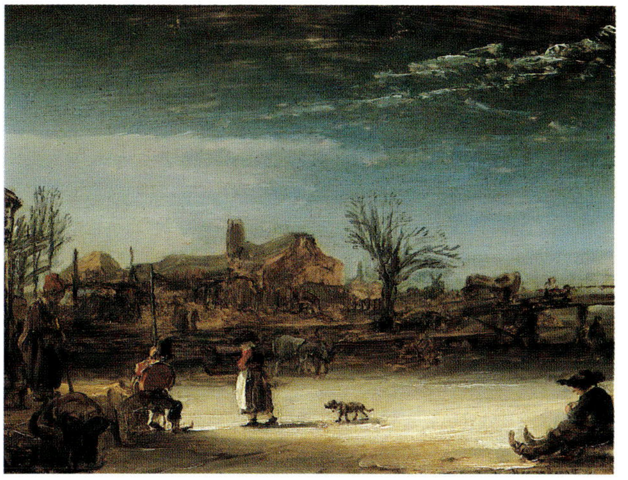

Rembrandt,
Winter Landscape

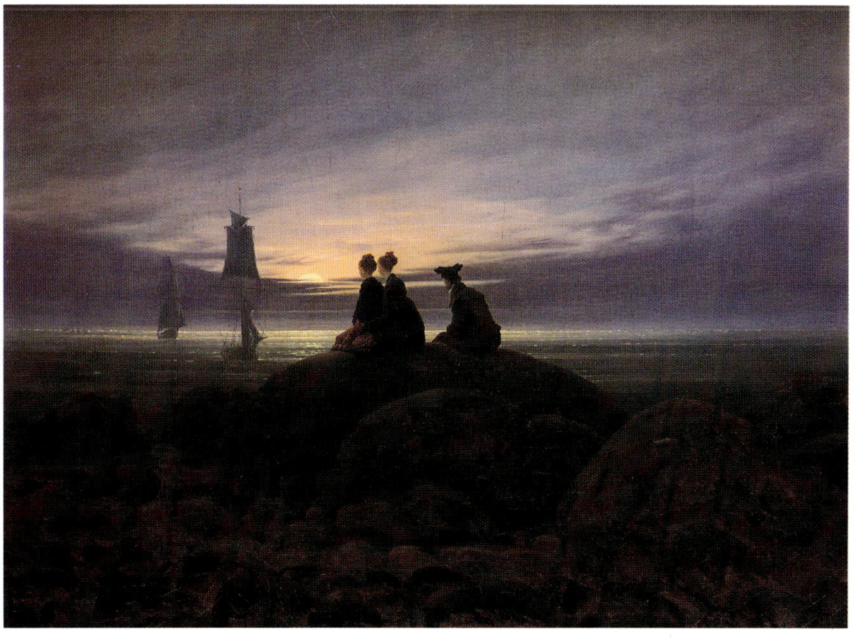

Caspar David Friedrich,
Moonrise over the Sea

The Impressionists, who painted in the late 1800's, approached landscape painting in a completely different manner. They were primarily interested in the influence of light and how it seemed to dissolve shapes. Claude Monet (1840-1926) created many studies from nature, and his paintings bear witness to a mastery of the colorful depiction of light.

Landscape painting has remained a fascinating motif, even today. The multifacetedness of nature, its spontaneity and transience, make it a timeless theme for any artist.

Idyllic pastoral scenes were popular motifs during the eighteenth century. Landscapes once again became stylized and formulaic. On the technical side, oil painting experienced an important advance with the automated production of oil paints. Artists no longer had to go to the trouble of mixing the paints themselves; instead, a standardized palette became available.

The depiction of nature has also changed through the centuries. Some artists rediscovered nature from a religious standpoint and viewed it primarily as a fantastic work of God. The German painter Caspar David Friedrich (1774-1840) subscribed to this Christian view of landscape painting. Thus, his paintings frequently depict the expanse and beauty of nature (and therefore of God) in contrast to the insignificance of man.

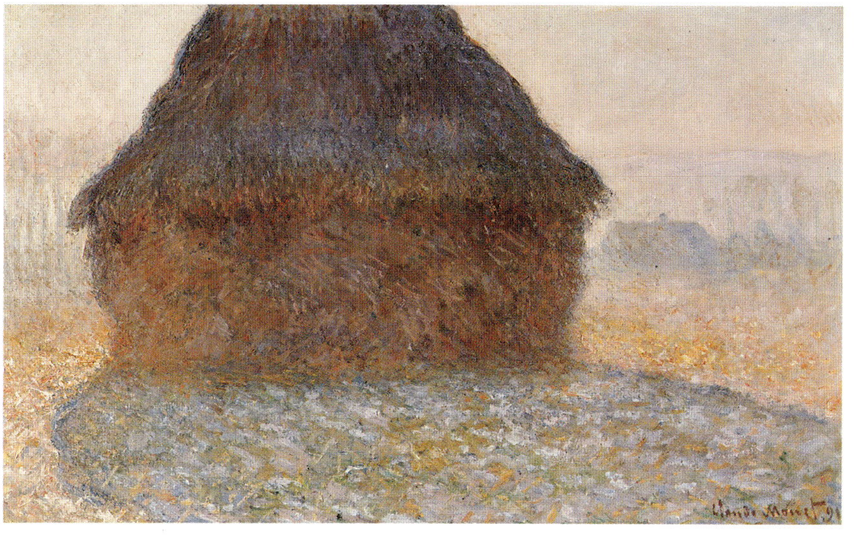

Claude Monet,
Haystack in the Sunlight

Choosing Materials

Good equipment is definitely an important prerequisite for successful oil paintings. It's best to invest in high-quality materials, even if it means buying less of them.

Prepackaged sets of materials are available in art supply stores and can be quite practical. These sets generally contain paints, brushes, a palette, turpentine, painting medium, and containers. The advantage of using prepackaged sets is that they are easy to carry. The disadvantage is that they are often more expensive than putting the materials together yourself.

If you decide to buy your materials separately, here are a few tips:

Let's start with the paints. High quality is of the utmost importance, and, when choosing colors, make sure they mix together well. At first, it will be enough to buy six to ten colors, which you can then use to mix other colors (see pages 12 and 13).

You won't always use the paints in the consistency in which they come out of the tube, so you'll need painting medium to thin them. Painting medium can also help the paint dry faster; it comes in three forms: slow-drying, medium-drying, and fast-drying.

If you paint a lot or on large surfaces, you might want to consider making your own oil paints. Oil pigments are available in powdered form, and you simply mix them with egg yolk and linseed oil or some other oil (you can also use resins or wax). It takes some experimentation to find a formula that works for you. If you're interested in mixing your own paints, see pages 50 and 51 for Christine Meder's "recipe."

Now on to brushes. Brushes should be sturdy and robust, so most oil painters choose bristle brushes. You can get them in round and flat varieties with bristles of varying lengths. Three or four brushes will be enough to start. Sable brushes are finer, and thus more delicate, and lend themselves to detailed work. These are also available in round and flat varieties. You have to clean sable brushes especially carefully, because the delicate hairs stick together easily. It is important that you clean your brushes as soon as you are done painting—unless, of course, you want to buy new brushes all the time. The simplest way to clean brushes is to use soap and lukewarm water while continuously lathering and rinsing the brush in the palm of your hand. You can also use turpentine or commercial brush cleaner, but a final washing in soap and water can't hurt. This sort of very thorough cleaning is necessary only if you won't be painting for a long period of time. If you take only a short break while you're working, you can put your brushes in clean water so they don't get stiff. Special holders for suspending the brushes in turpentine or water are very practical (see photo to the left of the easel). There are holders designed especially for oil painting that have a strainer to hold the sediment so the brushes always hang in clean turpentine or brush cleaner.

Palette and painting knives are useful for mixing paints on the palette, but they can also be used for scraping paint off the palette and applying it thickly on the canvas, as in the impasto technique.

You can buy canvases pre-primed, or you can prime them yourself (see pages 10 and 11). Blocks of individual sheets of painting paper, which you can tear off when you're through with a picture, are practical, but not cheap.

Instead of buying a palette, you might try using a piece of wood, plastic, or glass. You'll also need an easel if you want to paint on an upright canvas.

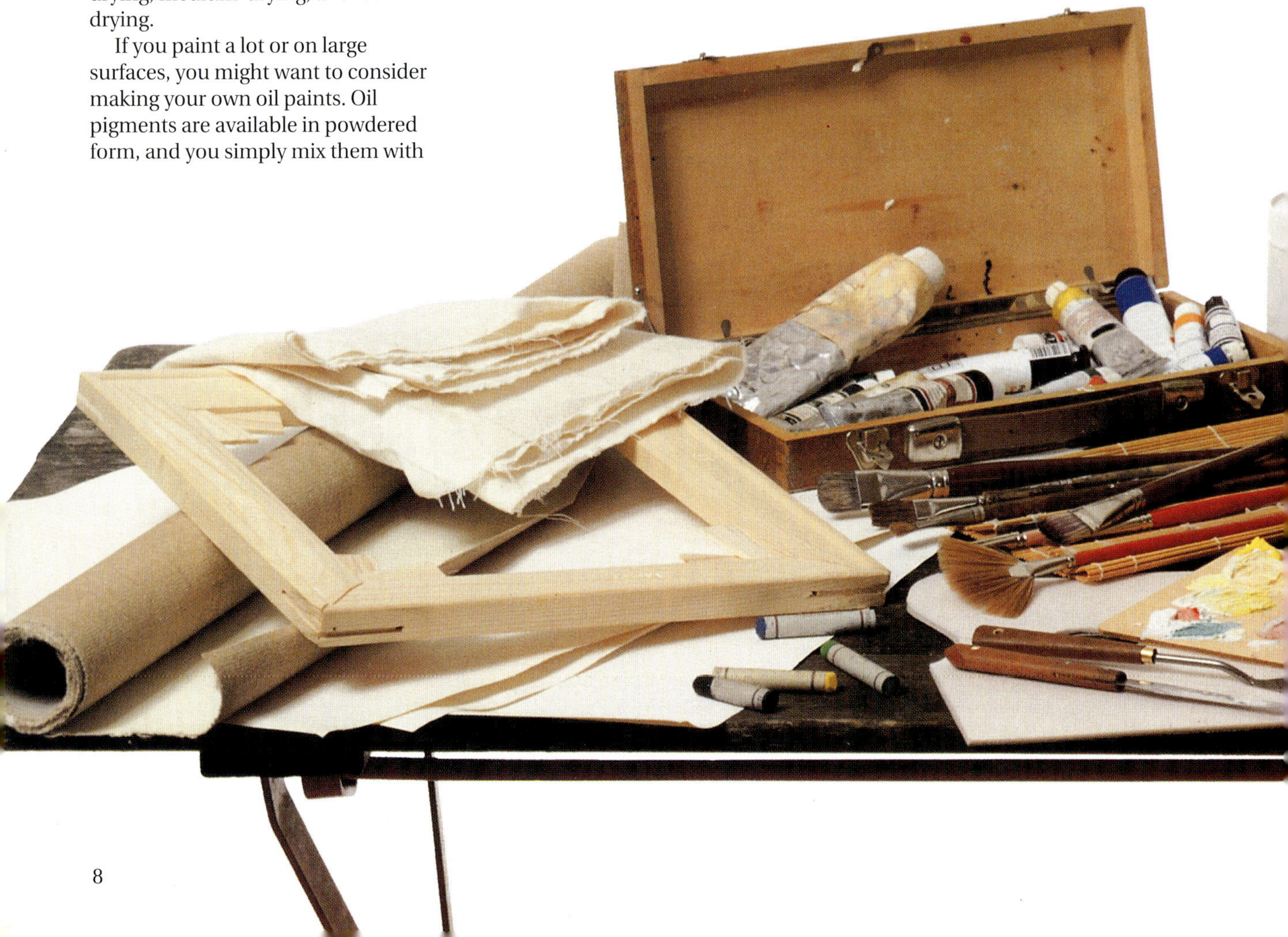

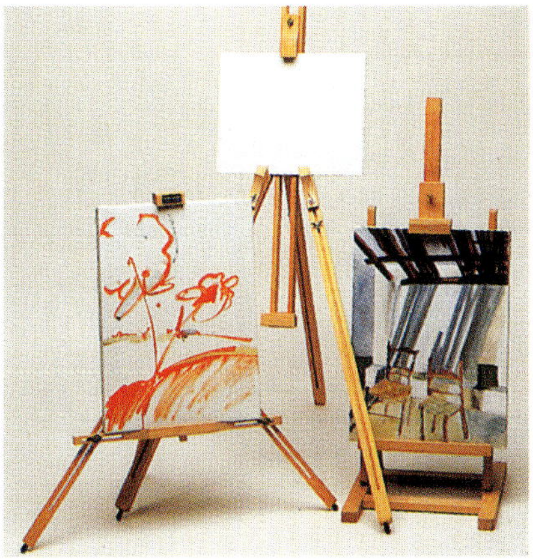

You can buy all different kinds of easels, ranging from small, which can be placed on a table, to large, which can stand on the floor or ground. Folding easels, which are easier to carry around and store (see photo below), are also available. In any case, don't be afraid to set up the easel in the store to see which type you're most comfortable with.

You'll also need a few rags to wipe up paint, and small containers for turpentine and painting medium. Some painters use wax crayons for preliminary sketches, but other artists prefer charcoal or a soft pencil. Finally, it's a good idea to wear a smock or an apron while you work. It's very easy to get paint on yourself, and oil paints are difficult to remove from clothing.

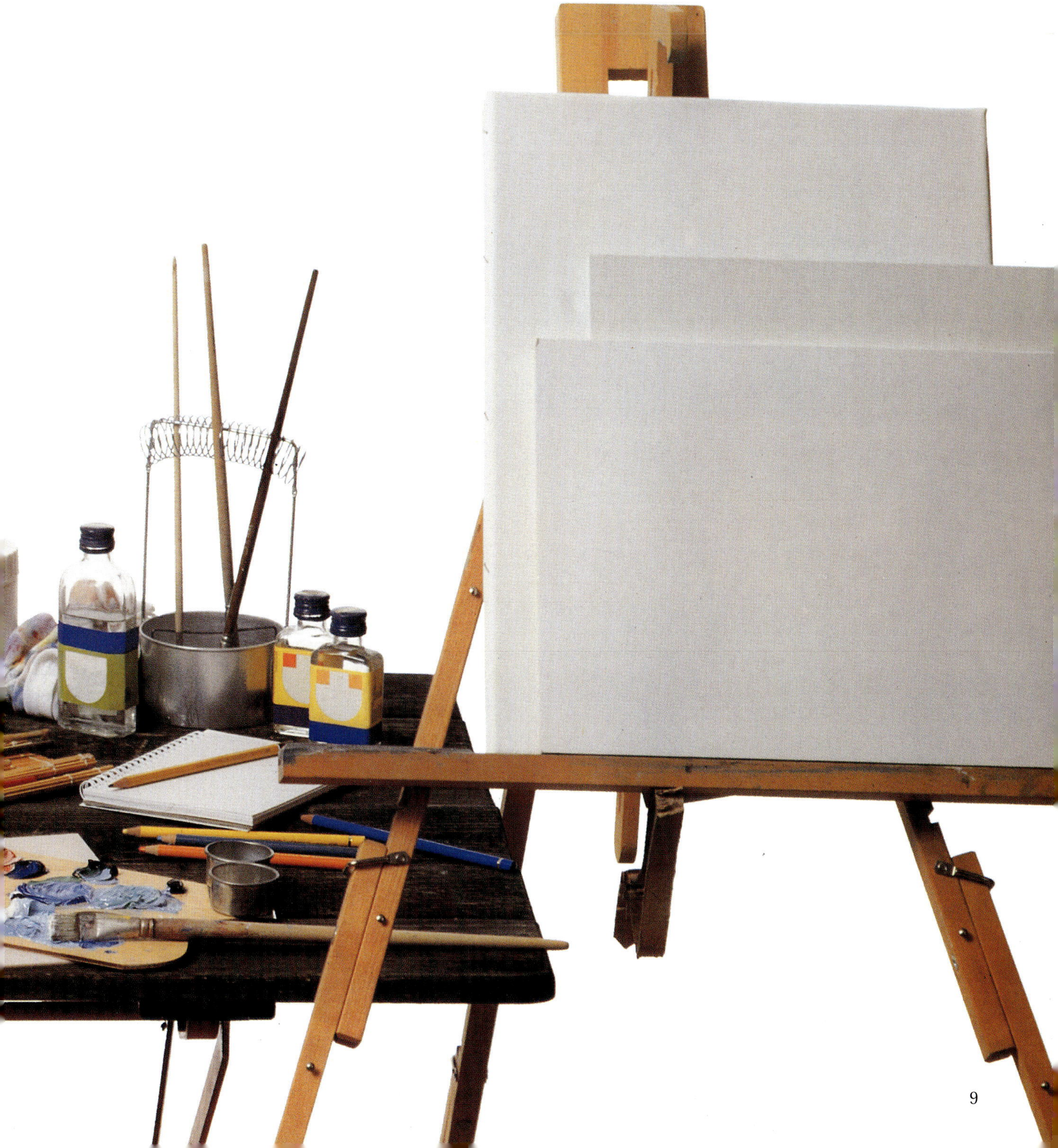

Preparation and Getting Started

Once you have all your materials and you've found a comfortable place to work, you will need to decide what type of surface you want to use. This is a very important step, because the surface has an effect on the expressiveness of your painting.

Stretching the Canvas

If prestretched canvases don't meet your needs, try your hand at building your own. The canvas material comes pre-primed or untreated for you to prime yourself. Cotton is best if you're doing your own priming. The frame that supports the canvas is made of pieces called "stretchers." Small wooden wedges called "corner keys" fit into the corners and allow the canvas to be tightened as necessary. If you don't have access to a workshop where you can cut precise angles with a saw, you should buy precut stretchers and corner keys at an art supply store (1).

When the stretchers are assembled, lay them on the canvas and cut the canvas so that about two inches extend beyond the frame. One side of each stretcher is cut at more of an angle so that it doesn't show through the canvas. Make sure the flat side is facing down.

After checking that the frame is parallel to the weave of the fabric, fold the canvas over one of the stretchers and tack or staple it to the center, then do the same on the opposite side. Repeat the process on the other two sides (2). Now you can stretch the rest. Always work from the center outward, alternating sides. Fold the corners neatly along the stretcher joint and nail them down (3). Since the canvas shrinks slightly after it's primed, don't stretch it too tightly. Otherwise, it will tear on the corners.

You will not need the corner keys until the primer has dried. There are slots in the stretchers where you can fit the corner keys. Carefully insert two keys per corner (4).

Painting Surfaces

Strictly speaking, you can work on any surface that doesn't buckle under the wet paint. It is very important, however, to make sure that the paints don't soak into the surface and leave ugly oily blotches. This can be avoided by properly priming the surface. You can see two examples of this in these illustrations at the bottom of the page.

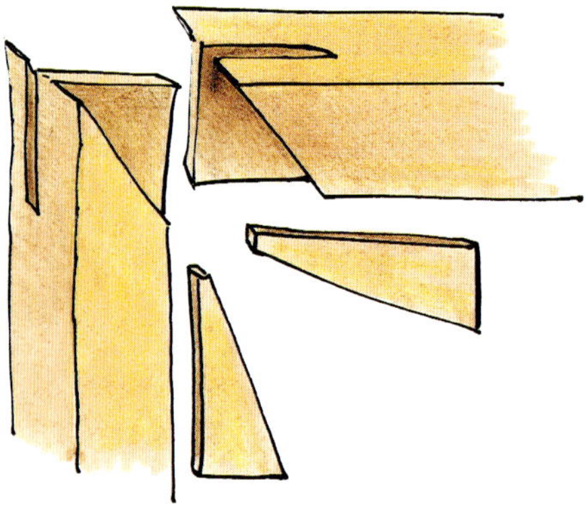

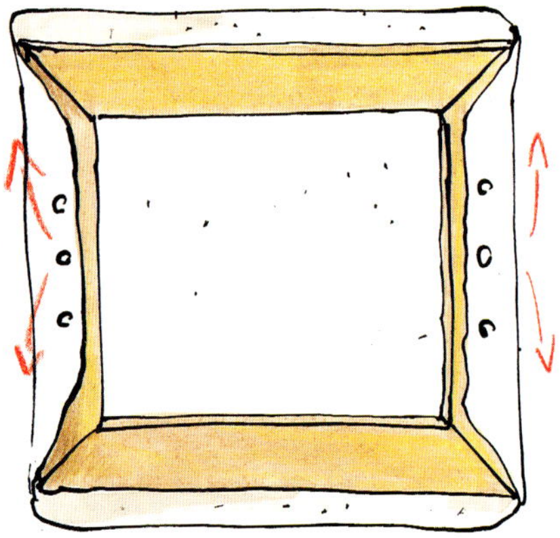

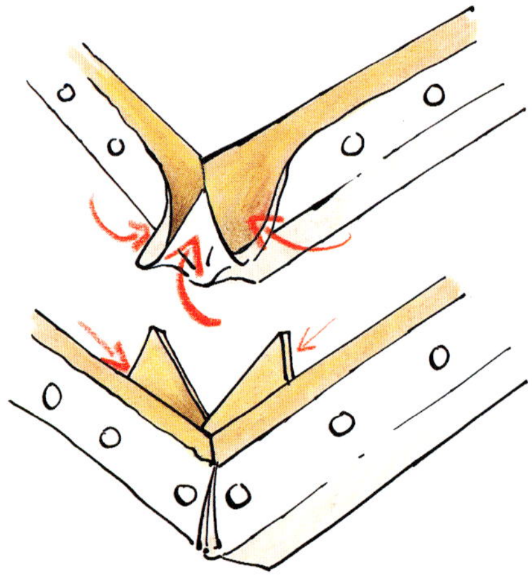

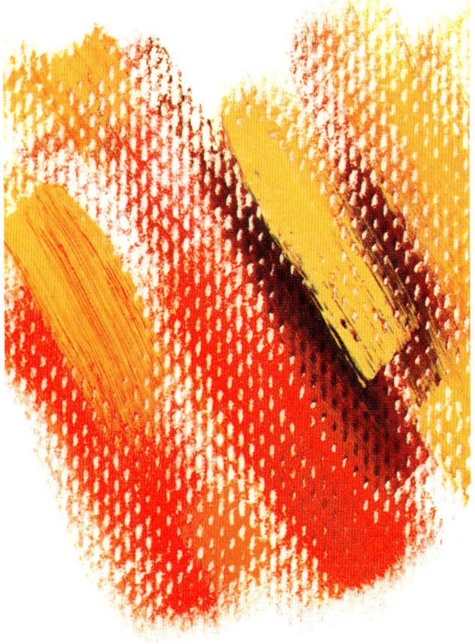

In the example on the left, a white primer was applied to thick, stretched watercolor paper, allowing the original texture to remain visible. You can also mix colors with the primer if you want. You can even use thinned oil paints as a primer, as was used on the thick blue cardboard to the right. Be warned, however, that not all surfaces are lasting, even when primed properly. For example, an oil painting done on primed watercolor paper will deteriorate over time.

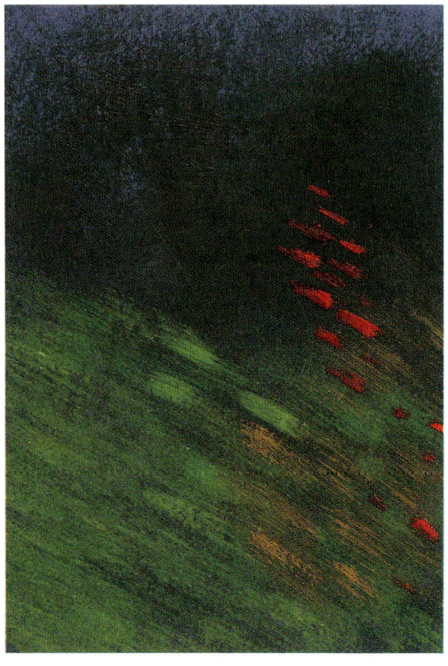

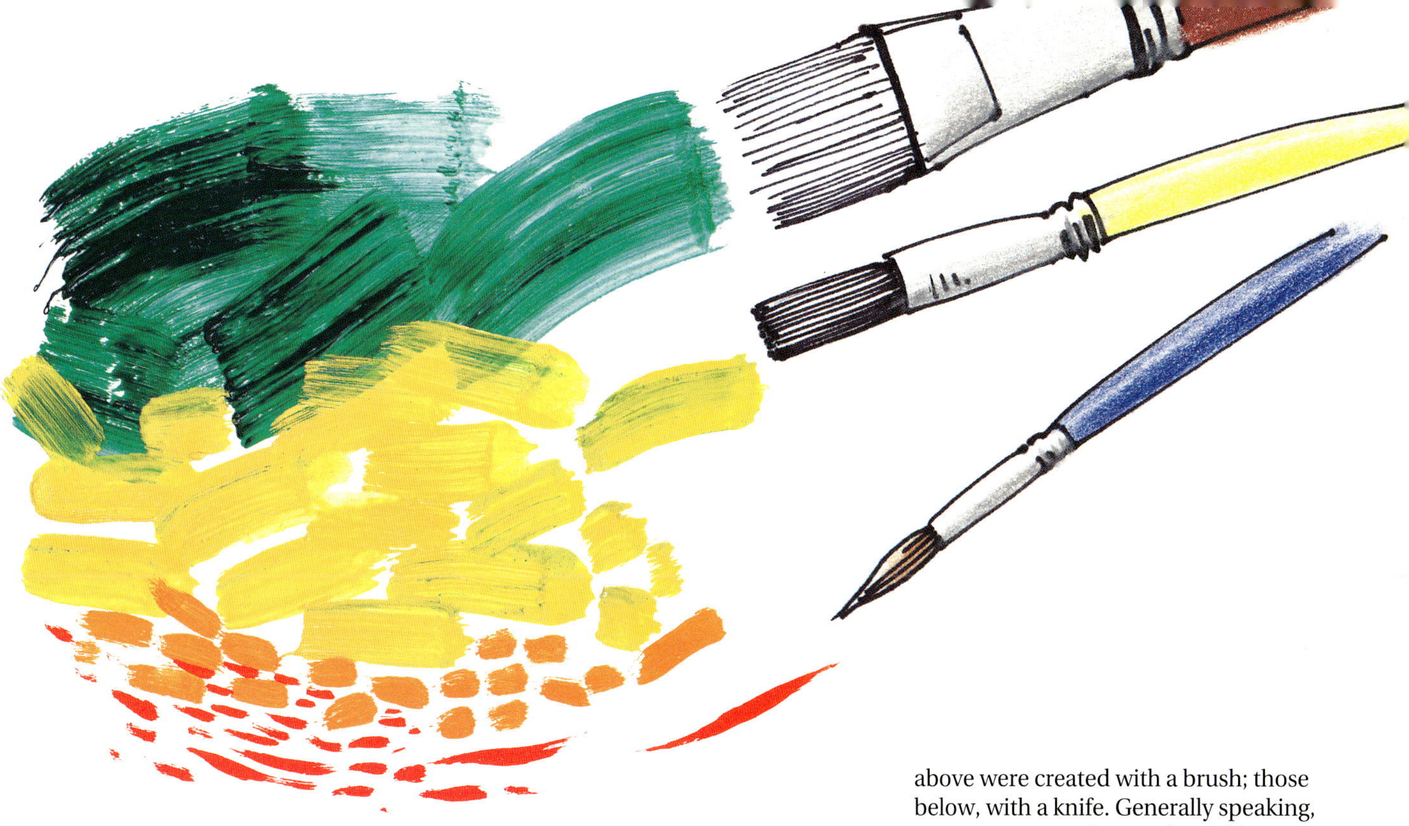

If you paint on odd-sized canvases and do not want to go to the trouble of stretching them yourself, you can always have canvases built to your specifications at art supply stores.

Untreated canvas should be primed with polymer Gesso or it will soak up a lot of paint. Gesso is a white primer that can be applied thick and textured or thin and smooth—it depends on the type of surface you want for your painting.

Brushes and Knives

The type of picture you want to paint will determine whether to use a knife or a brush. Soft, round brushes are better for intricate, detailed motifs. A broad, flat brush or a knife typically lends itself to heavily textured applications or large areas of paint. As always, the choice is up to you. The illustrations shown here are just some of the effects that are possible with these tools. The examples above were created with a brush; those below, with a knife. Generally speaking, you can create softer strokes with longer bristles, and shorter bristles leave a more obvious brush texture. Flat brushes can result in a very lively stroke if you twist the brush while you're painting—but you can also use them to achieve hard edges and precise lines. Round brushes are good for painting soft, flowing lines.

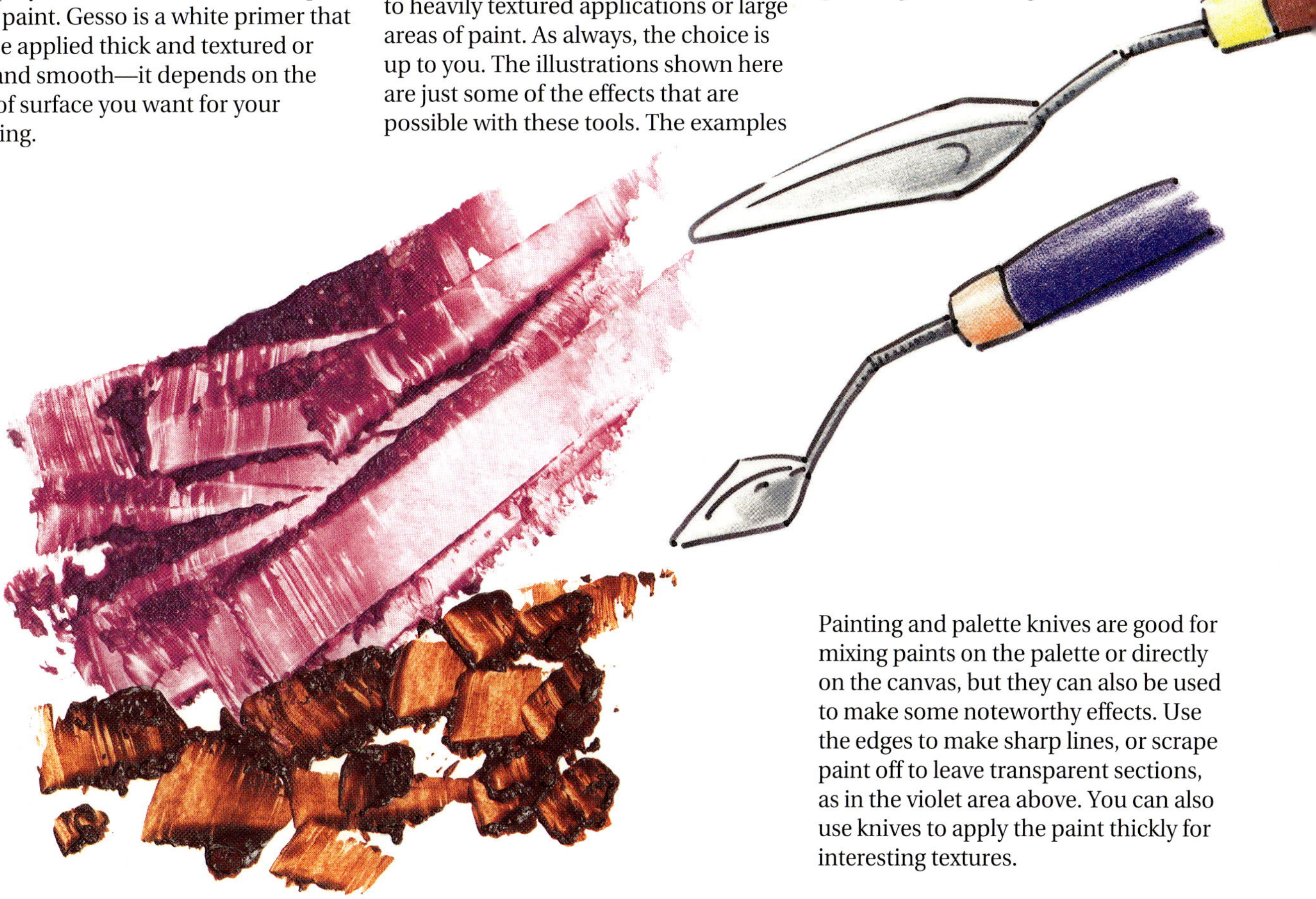

Painting and palette knives are good for mixing paints on the palette or directly on the canvas, but they can also be used to make some noteworthy effects. Use the edges to make sharp lines, or scrape paint off to leave transparent sections, as in the violet area above. You can also use knives to apply the paint thickly for interesting textures.

Mixing Oil Paints

You can create a surprising number of hues with just a few basic colors. The best way to get a feel for mixing colors is by practicing.

The example below shows a small selection of colors that are particularly suitable for landscape painting and that can be mixed to produce a wide variety of other hues. You can use white to lighten colors, but it also makes them appear cooler, while colors darkened with black seem warmer. So be careful! If you use too much black and white for mixing, your colors quickly become gray and muddy.

If you look closely at the palette shown below, you'll see that black has not even been included. Many painters think black is too harsh. Besides, there is no black in nature—the impression of black is created by the absence of light.

You can make your own black very easily. Mix equal parts of alizarin crimson, burnt umber, and chromium oxide green. If you change the amount of any one of these colors, the black you end up with will also change. If you do want to use a commercial black, ivory black is recommended.

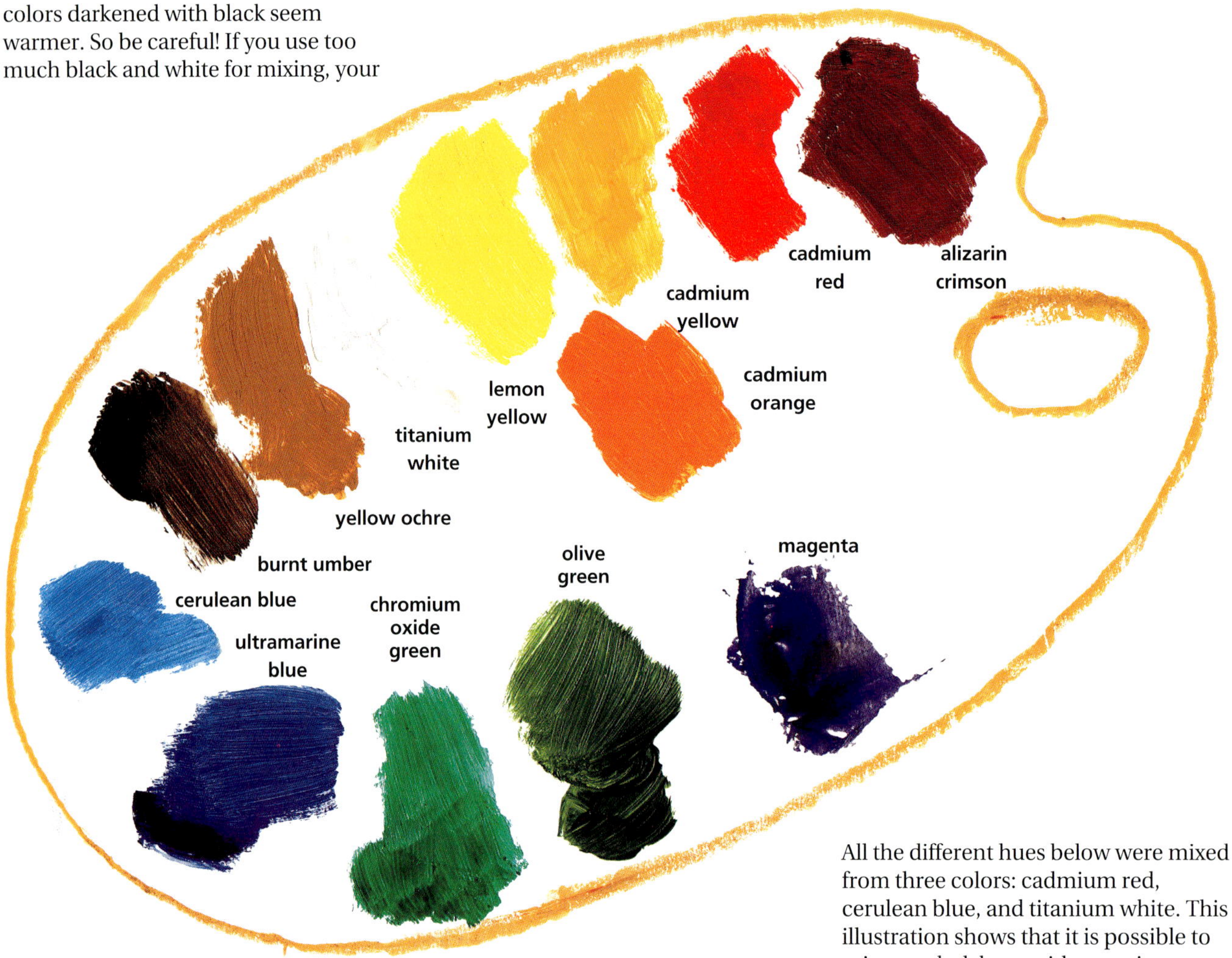

All the different hues below were mixed from three colors: cadmium red, cerulean blue, and titanium white. This illustration shows that it is possible to mix very dark hues without using any black at all.

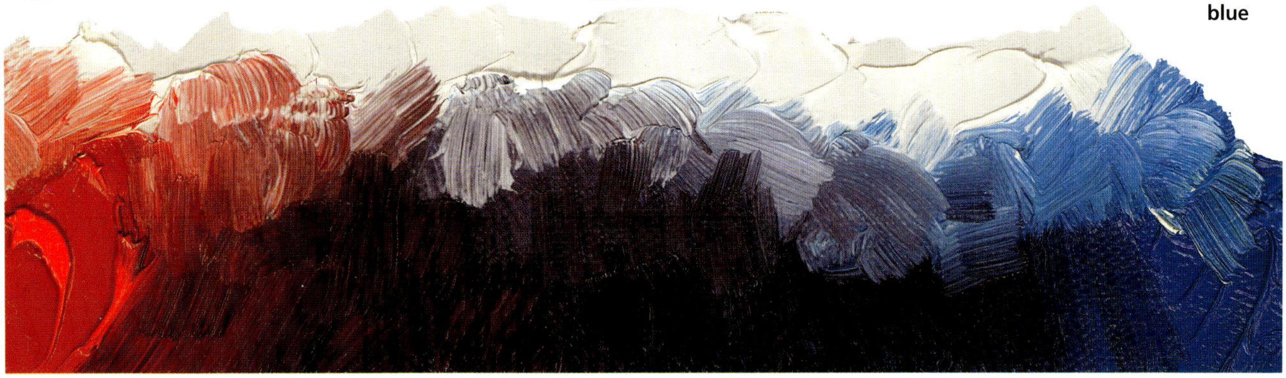

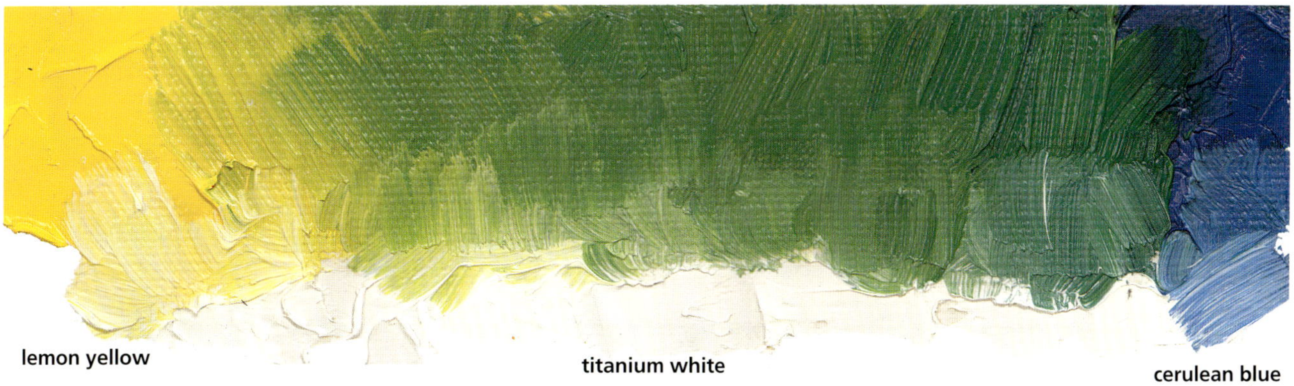

We can find all different kinds of greens in nature, and they are constantly changing under the effects of light and shadow. It often seems impossible to capture them all in a painting. But remember that you also have a huge selection of greens at your disposal. An unbelievable number of nuances can be created just from cerulean blue, lemon yellow, and titanium white (above). Try mixing some of the other blues, yellows, and greens shown in the palette on page 12.

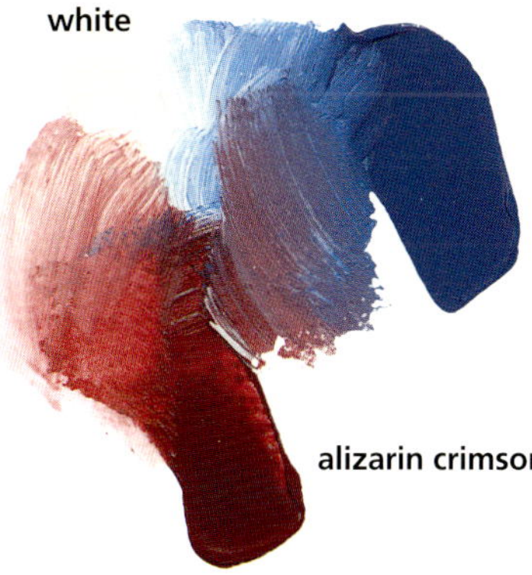

Here are a few more mixtures to give you some ideas. They were all created using colors from the palette on page 12. Mixing colors just for practice may seem boring to you, but it has two distinct advantages: first, you gain more confidence in handling colors; second, you can create a file containing successful mixtures and descriptions of how you created them.

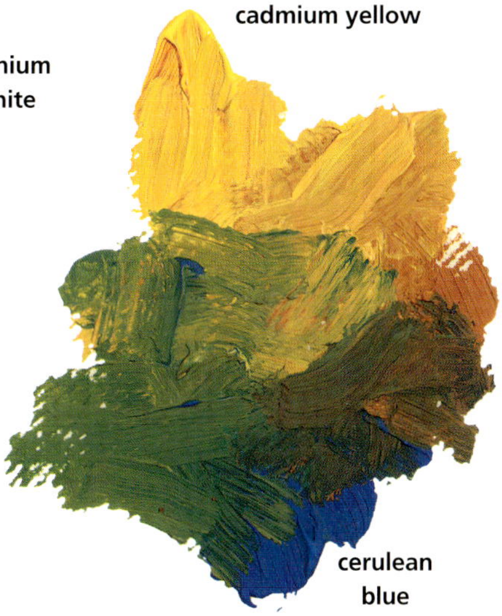

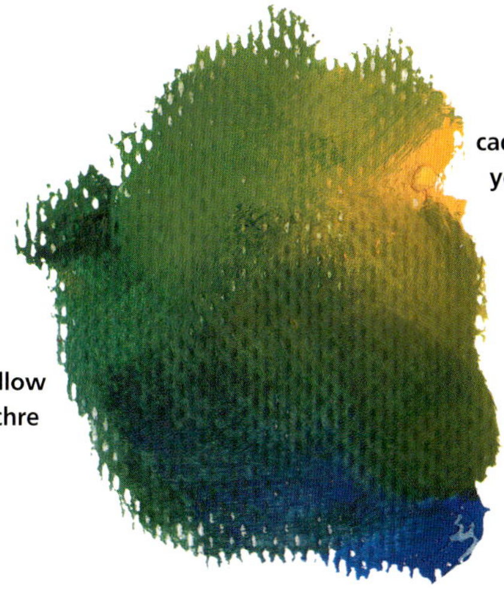

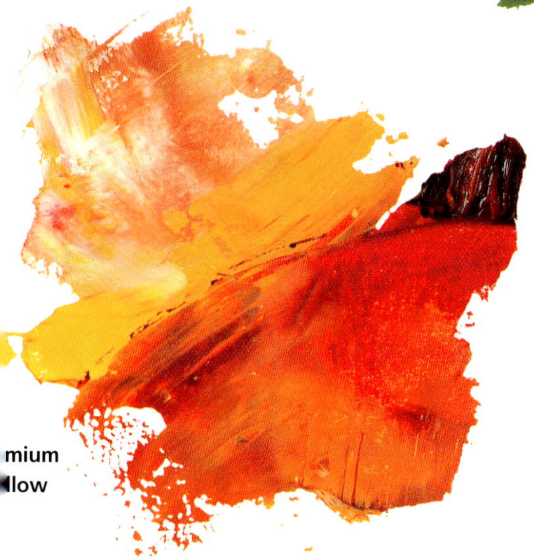

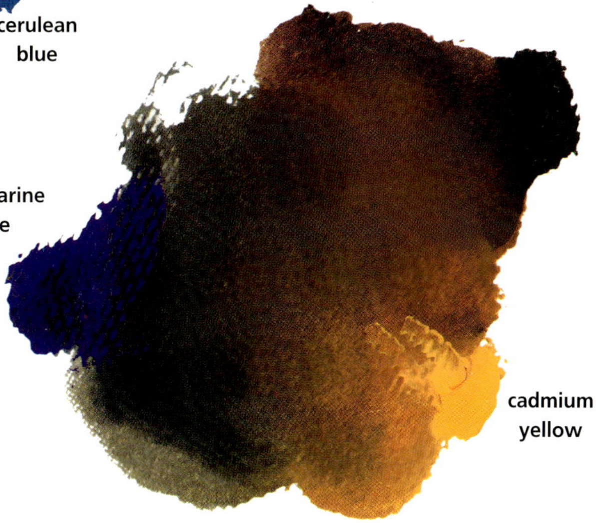

The Techniques of Oil Painting

As in all types of painting, there are certain basic techniques you need to be familiar with when you paint in oils. This doesn't mean that you shouldn't experiment, though. The only way to find out which way of painting you like the most is to try them all out.

A special feature of oil paints is that they keep a long time. This also means that they take a long time to dry. If you squeeze paint onto the palette and then take a break—be it for a few days or a few weeks—you can reuse the paint. Unthinned paint dries the slowest. If you thin the paint with painting medium, you can accelerate the drying time. Mixing the paint with linseed oil or turpentine will also speed up the drying time, but not as drastically as with painting medium.

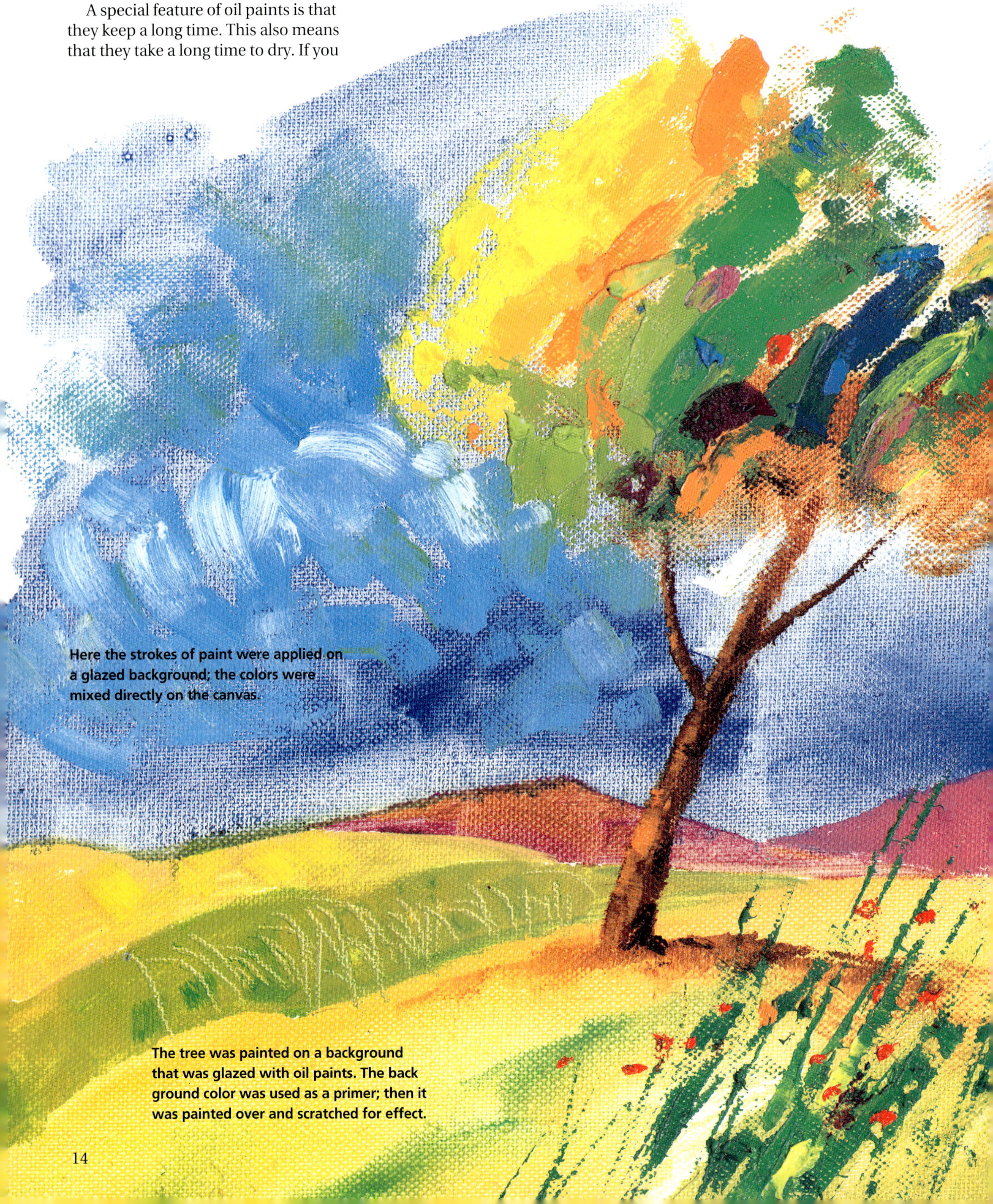

Here the strokes of paint were applied on a glazed background; the colors were mixed directly on the canvas.

The tree was painted on a background that was glazed with oil paints. The back ground color was used as a primer; then it was painted over and scratched for effect.

Applying Glazes

A glaze is a thin layer of paint that allows the background to shimmer through, whether it's canvas or another color. Be careful when you're working with several layers of paint: If you want to prevent the color underneath from mixing with the fresh paint, it has to be completely dry.

Working Wet-in-Wet

If you apply wet paint on top of wet paint, the colors mix directly on the canvas. Oil paints, however, don't run randomly or flow into one another, as watercolors do. You have much more control over the oil paint mixture.

Working Dry-on-Dry

You can get interesting textures by applying a little paint to a dry background, as in the right portion of the treetop in the example below. The dry brush stroke allows the background to show through and leaves its own texture. In the example to the upper right, you can see a combination of the wet-in-wet and dry-on-dry effects.

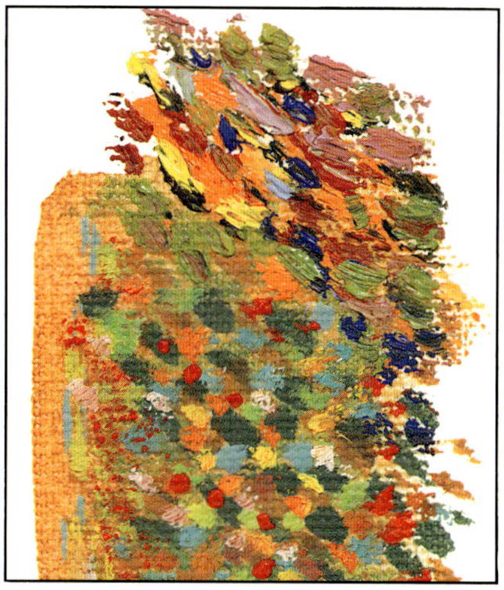

Painting Gradations

Behind the hills, you can see a gradation from dark blue to light blue to white. In this case, the artist simply increased the amount of white added to the darker color, but you could also do it the opposite way. You can paint smooth gradations using even brush strokes from top to bottom (or vice versa), or, as in the area to the left of the tree, heavily textured gradations with visible brush strokes.

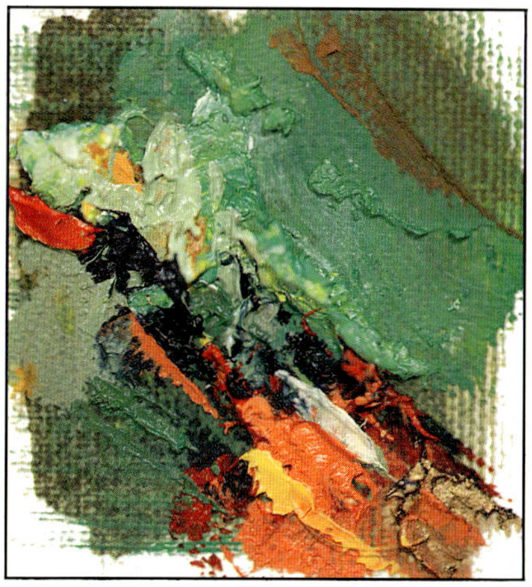

Using Impasto

The impasto technique involves applying thick layers of paint that result in a raised texture (see the example above). The texture can be so pronounced that you can feel it with your hand. You can achieve this effect using a stiff brush or a palette knife. When the paint sticks up from the surface, it creates "plasticity." Depending on the concentration of the paint, the drying process can last quite some time, even several months. Remember—fresh paint won't "stand up" very well because of its oil content. To avoid this, first squeeze the paint onto a paper towel so the excess oil is absorbed, then apply the stiffer paint that results.

Using the Knife

Knives are handy for applying large areas of color or heavy textures (see the treetop). You can actually "paint" directly on the canvas with the knife; it works especially well for drawing sharp edges, as you can see in the blades of grass.

The Expressive Aspect of Color

You've probably noticed, while mixing your colors, that you like some hues more than others. We tend to associate certain colors with particular moods—they remind us of pleasant or unpleasant feelings or experiences. Warm and cool colors are a simple example of this. Ice, snow, and frost appear blue, so we associate blue with cold. Fire and the sun, on the other hand, seem red, yellow, or orange, so we associate these colors with warmth. Of course, this classification is not always clear-cut, since there are also warm blues and cool reds.

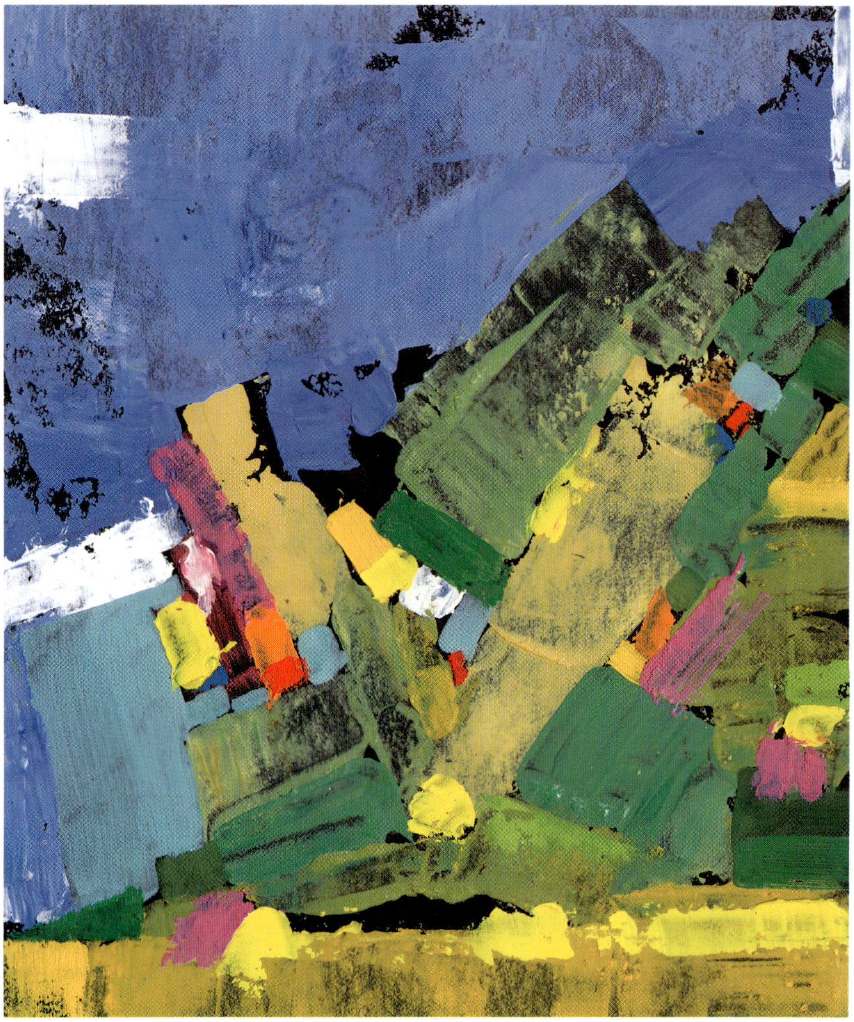

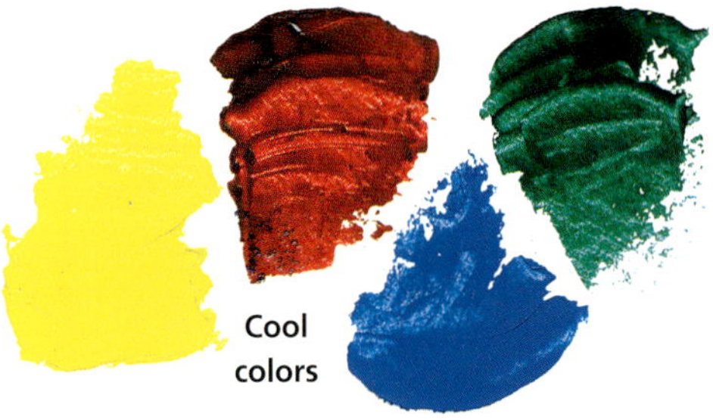

Cool colors

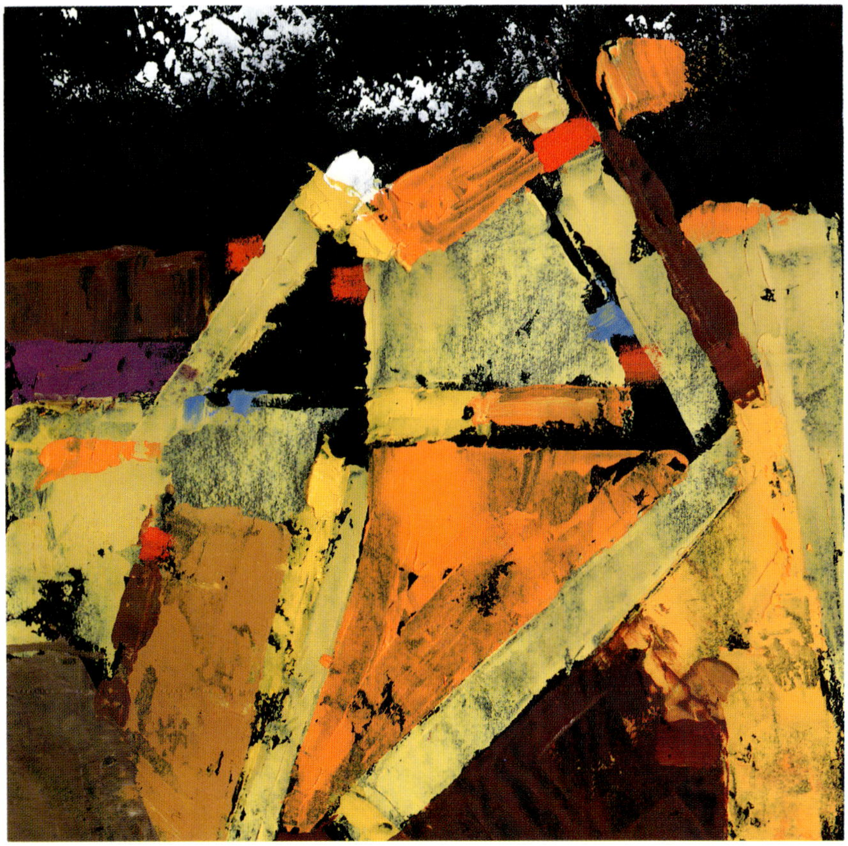

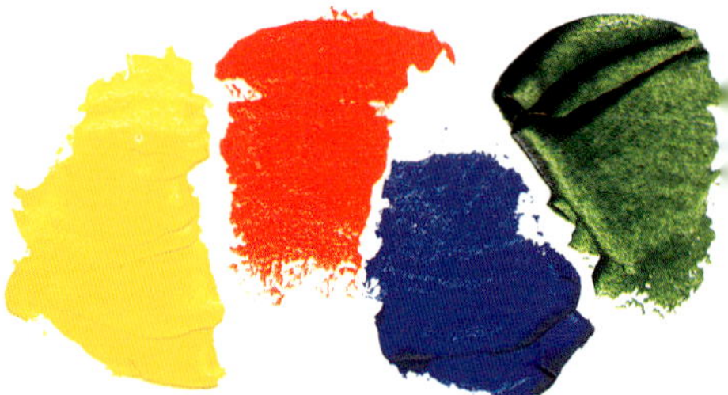

Warm colors

Generally speaking, colors with a predominantly blue content seem cool, and colors with a predominantly red content appear warm.

Colors can express a broad spectrum of emotions—they can seem happy, sad, aggressive, or melancholy. You don't even need a happy or sad motif in order to create these impressions—the colors alone are enough. This effect is demonstrated in the four abstract compositions shown here, in which the characteristic colors of the four seasons are captured.

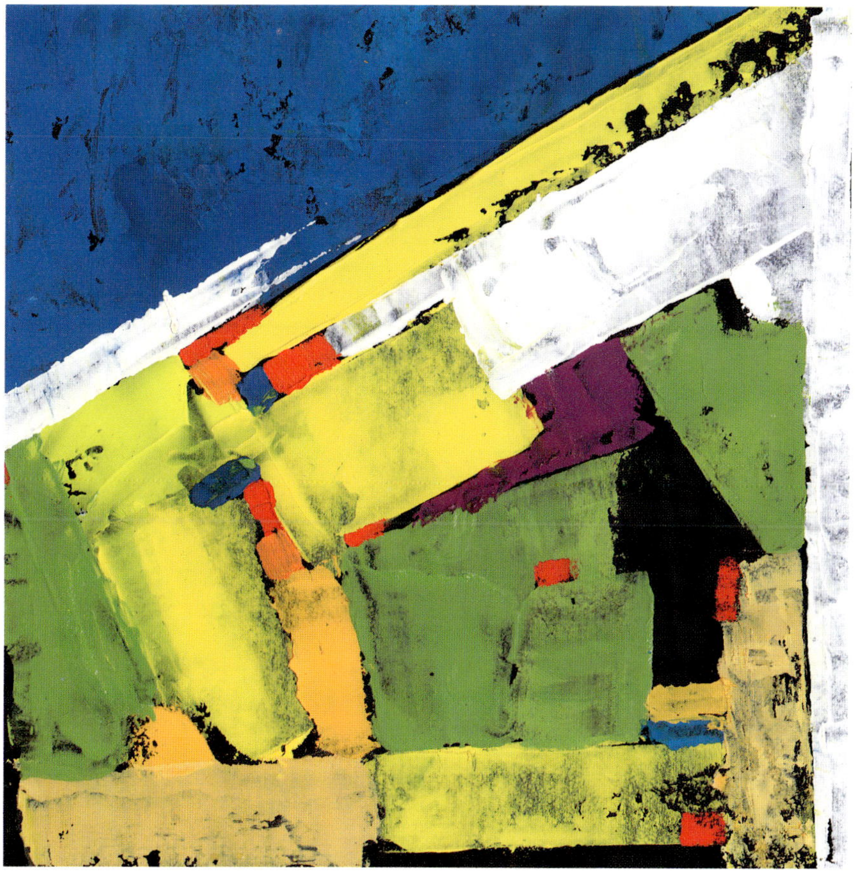

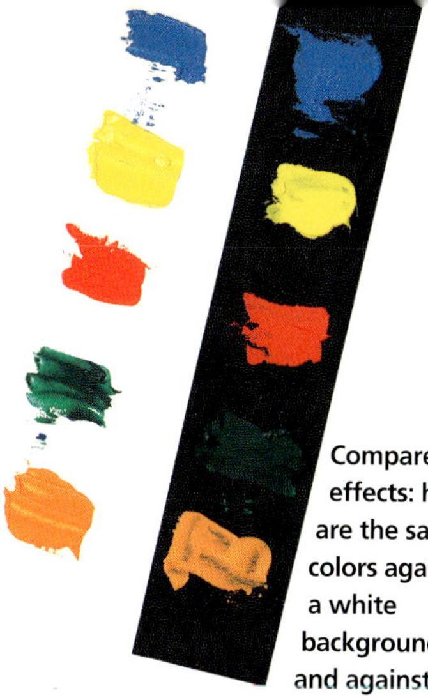

Compare the effects: here are the same colors against a white background and against a black background.

Of course, cool colors and mostly blues were used for winter (below). Notice how the white looks even cooler due to the blue mixed in with it. The interesting thing is that the "cold" effect becomes even more pronounced when contrasted with a warm color, as in the dark red on the white in this example (or vice versa, as in the cool blue with the warm ochres in the autumn composition).

A black background was used here because it makes the foreground colors seem particularly brilliant. A white painted against a black background seems "whiter" than, for example, one painted against a blue background.

Although each person perceives the seasons differently, each season has typical characteristics. Spring, for example, contains the first delicate greens of the year and perhaps the yellows and pinks of the first buds. Autumn, on the other hand, contains the reddish browns and golds of the changing leaves.

The illustration at the top of the opposite page shows the spring composition. You can feel the delicate colors of the blossoms, but the browns left over from the bare trees of winter still show through.

In summer (above), the colors become more pronounced. The green is more brilliant, illuminated by the sun, the blue gives the impression of a summer sky, and the yellows and reds have a warm effect. This example also shows how the various colors affect one another, how they accentuate or overpower other colors.

Rust colors were chosen for autumn (opposite). Warm colors dominate, because autumn still has some of the warmth of summer.

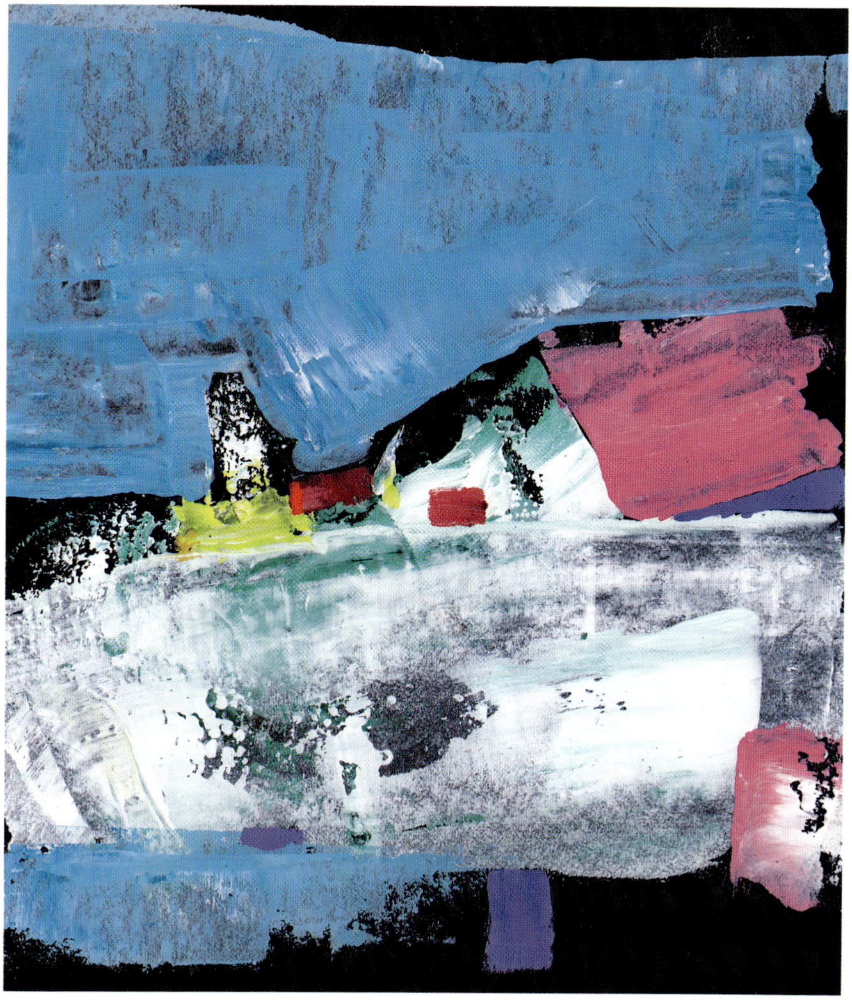

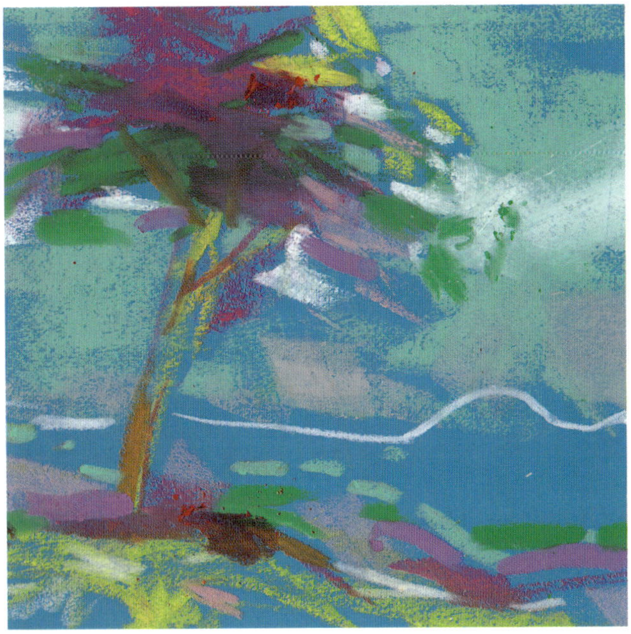

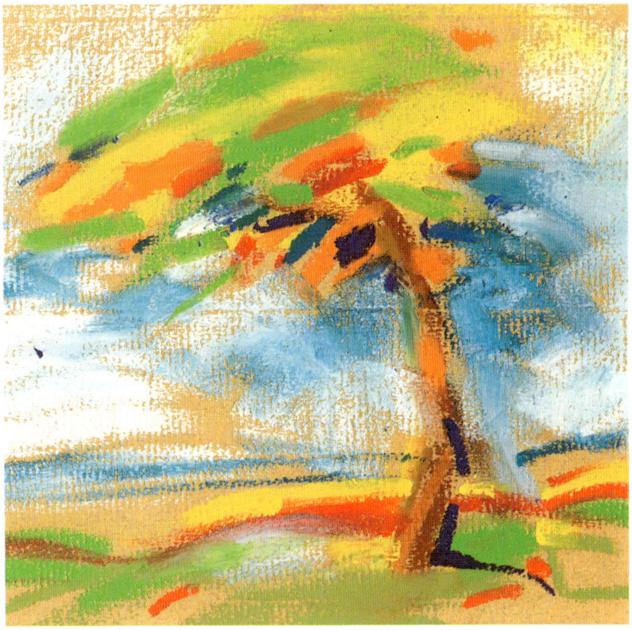

Now let's get a little more abstract. Although the two pictures above contain the same motif—a tree with a landscape in the background—each one expresses a completely different mood.

The picture on the left has been painted in cool colors, giving it a more melancholy effect. The delicate pastels, the blue background, and the purples and the cool greens are responsible for this.

The ochre-colored background in this picture, on the other hand, creates a warm mood, which is emphasized by the other colors. The same tree, now shown before a more peaceful landscape, has a livelier, happier effect. The entire painting radiates warmth, and this effect is accentuated by a few contrasting cool colors.

Try an exercise like this yourself. Find a simple motif, sketch it in different color combinations, and observe how the mood of your painting changes.

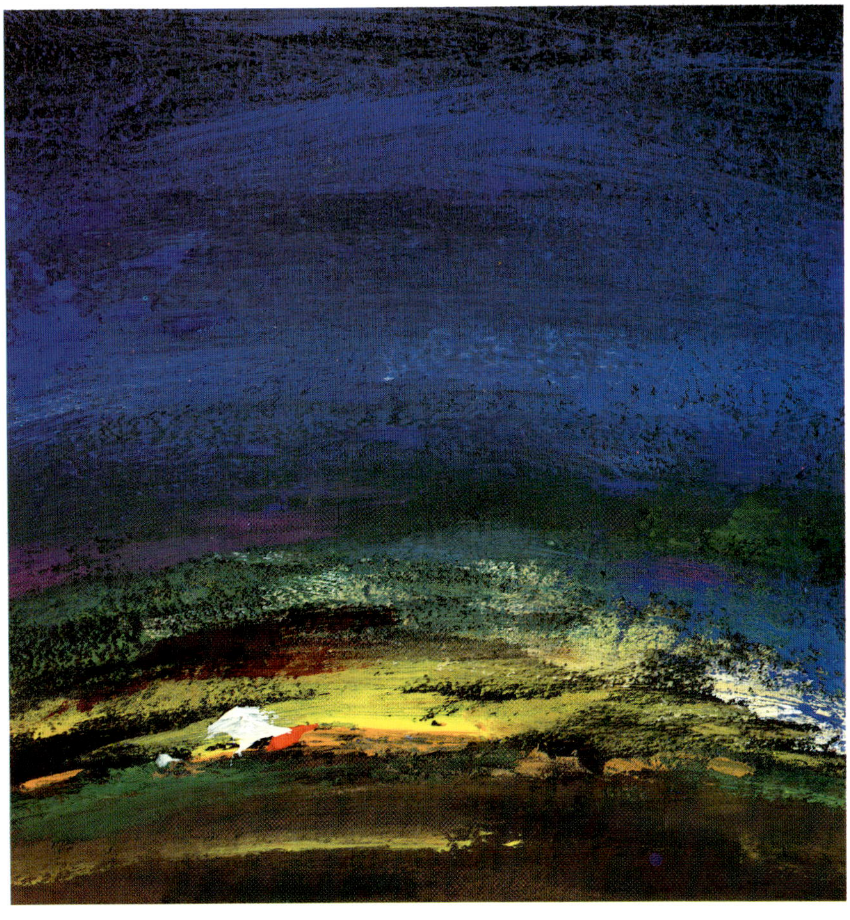

Painting Sky and Clouds

Depending on the weather, and thus on the distribution of light and shadow, colors can appear powerful or weak. The wind not only blows bushes, trees, and grass, but also the clouds. Even a cloudless sky contains different colors—it's not just an even blue. In contrast to watercolor painting, in which the paints often form cloud-like shapes on their own, when painting in oils, you have to consciously model each cloud and each portion of the sky. The simplest way to paint a cloudless sky is to apply a glaze, letting the background show through. To illustrate this effect, the artist chose a black background again and applied blue mixed with a little white. In this way, the cloudless sky doesn't look as if it has been painted; it holds drama and interest.

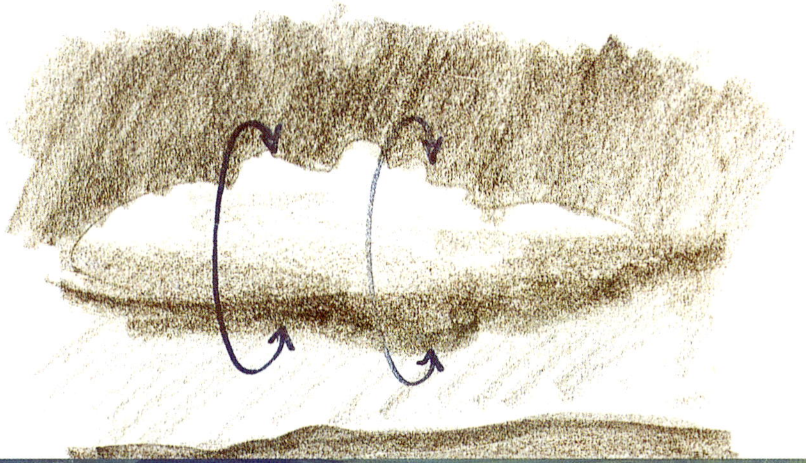

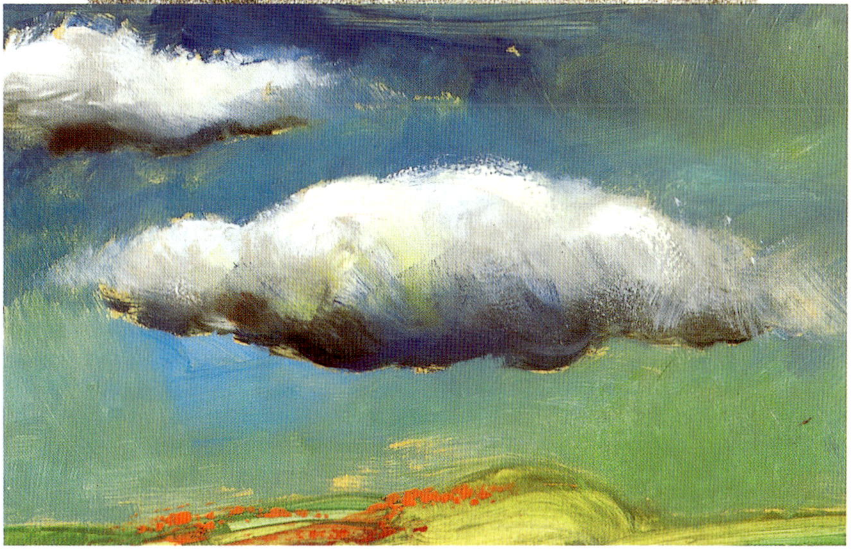

Unfortunately, there's no recipe for painting clouds. The best way to do it is to observe them closely and practice painting them. Look out the window when it's storming or when little clouds are beginning to form. Observe the changes in color and shape, and analyze the dark and light values.

Generally speaking, clouds are darker on the bottom than on the top. There are almost always white areas, even in storm clouds, and they help give the clouds shape. Simple black-and-white sketches will help you get an idea of where to put the dark and light values (above). Then you can transfer your sketch to oils. It's okay if the warm color of the background (yellow ochre) shows through. When it is time to paint the clouds themselves, it is best to stick to the dark and light values developed in your sketch. In the painting to the left, a dry brush was used to add the white highlights and the yellow in the ground.

The illustration below shows a picture of slowly forming clouds. The white was applied in a dry-brush glaze over the dark blue.

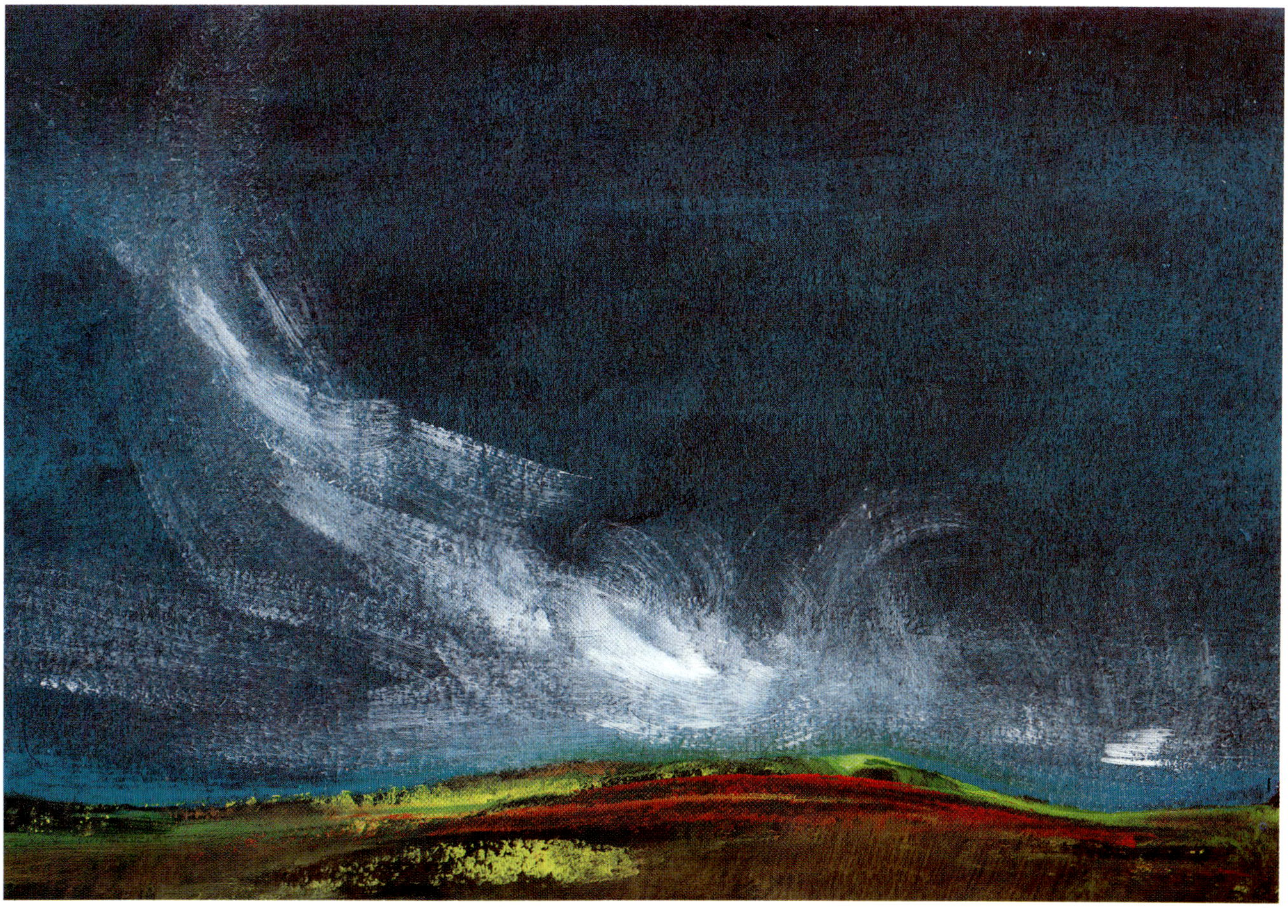

Learning to See

It is not always easy to transfer what you see to a piece of paper. When you are painting a landscape motif, you often have to leave out certain things—after all, you can't paint each blade of grass or each individual leaf. This is why it is very important to know how to simplify what you see. Many objects can be reduced to three basic shapes: the rectangle, the circle, and the triangle. A tree, for example, can be drawn as a narrow rectangle for the trunk and a circle for the top.

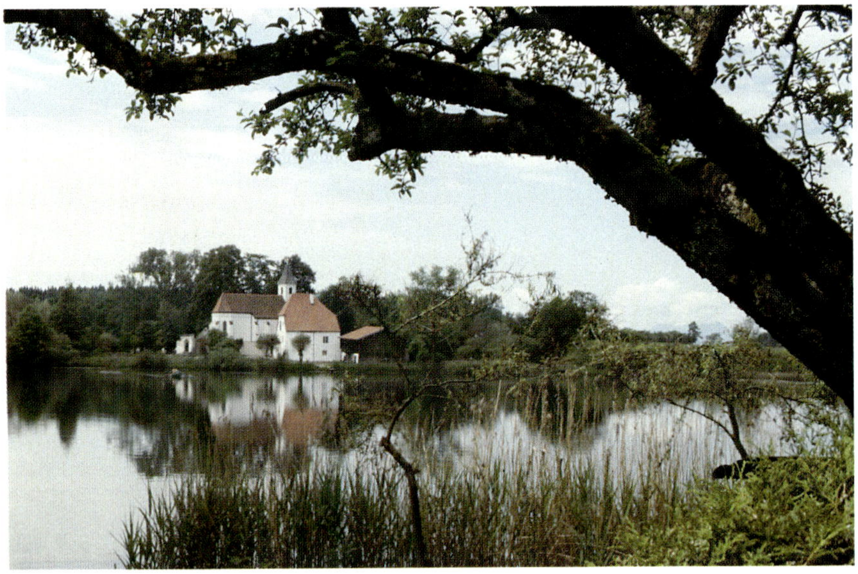

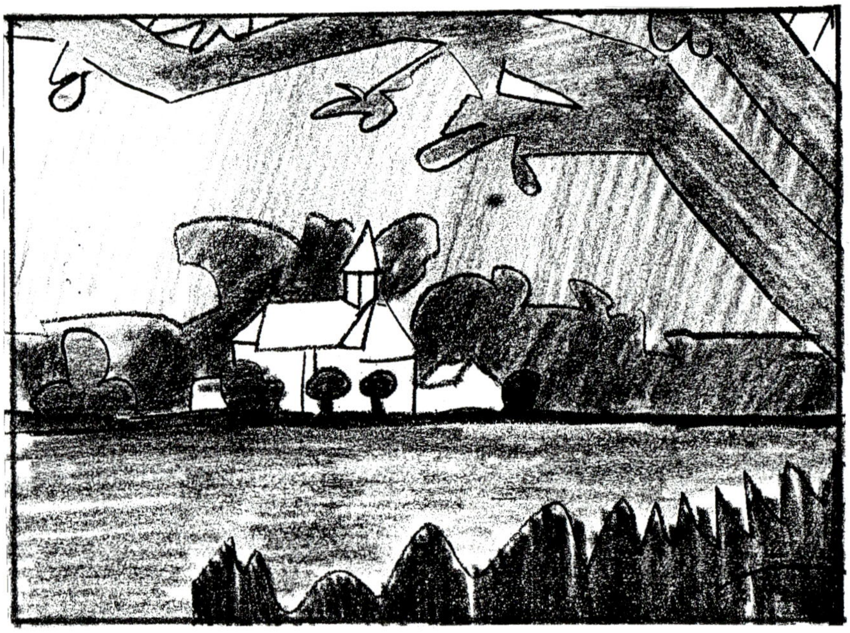

The first thing you have to do when you find a motif is decide what is important and what you can leave out. For example, you might want to leave out a telephone line or make a plant larger. This freedom is one advantage painting has over photography.

Let's use the photo shown above as an example. The important elements were identified and reduced to their basic shapes. The black-and-white sketch at the left helped the artist work out the sizes of the objects and find the focal point of the picture. Many artists make more than one preliminary sketch.

Here the artist tried different variations. The trees and the meadow were minimized, and the accent was put on the church and the buildings. In order to retain some of the impression of distance, part of the tree and the branches were positioned in the foreground. A few areas of color were applied to get a feel for the dark and light values, but the colors themselves weren't necessarily indicative of the colors that would be used in the final painting.

As an exercise, choose three sections of this photo and sketch them. You can exaggerate certain elements, add others, or leave some out entirely.

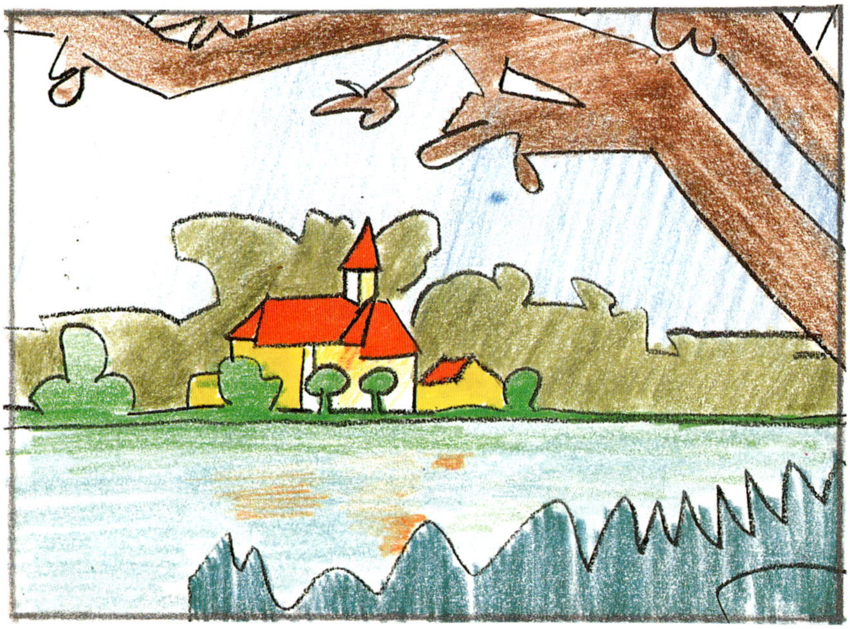

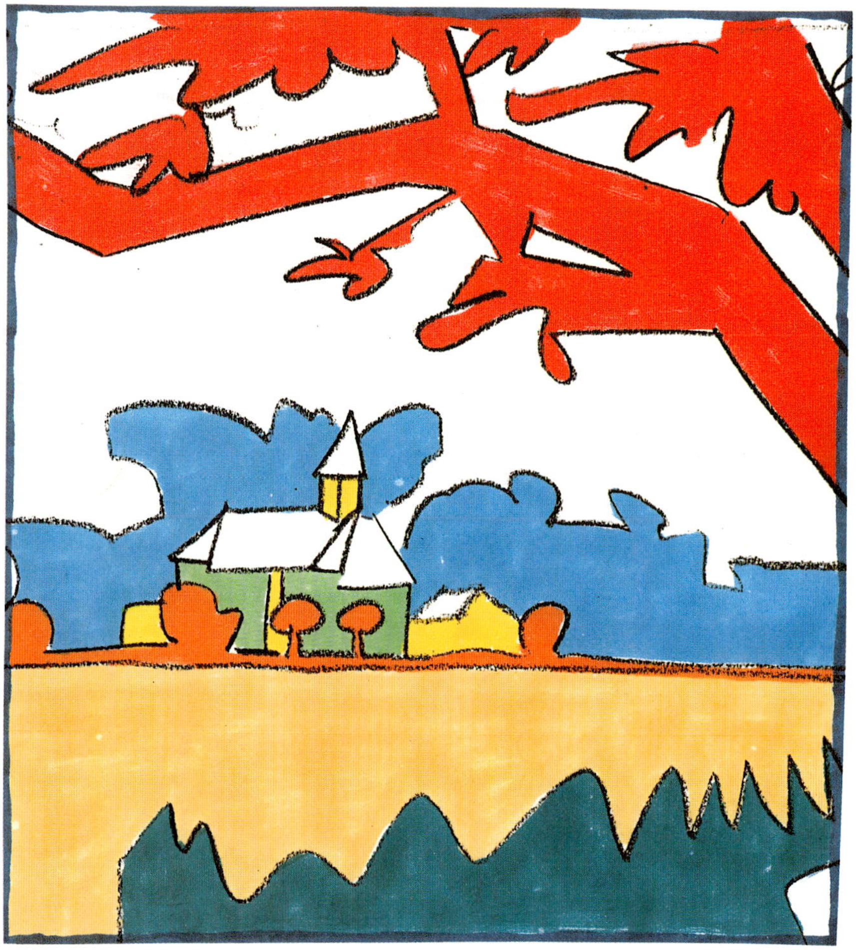

The negative space (the space between the objects in a motif) is just as important as the positive space (the shapes of the objects themselves). You can see this very clearly in the two examples at the left. The tree, the church, and the plants are important for the composition, as are the shapes between these objects (in this case, the sky and the water). Negative space can complement the positive space or dominate it, so you have to plan shapes, sizes, and colors very carefully.

Which part of the picture was this shape taken from? You can find it in both the top and the bottom picture, and the color scheme makes it seem either positive or negative.

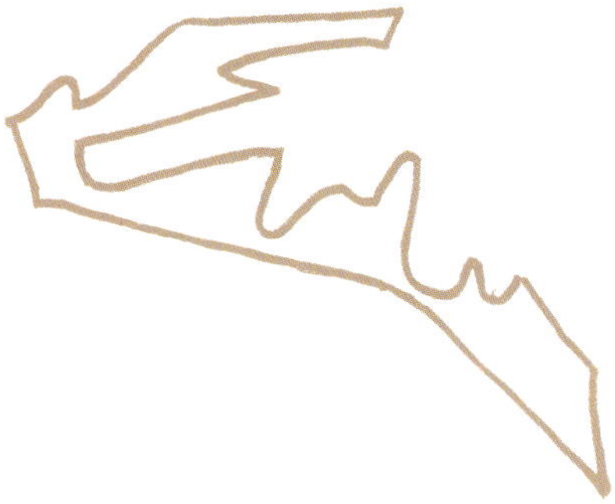

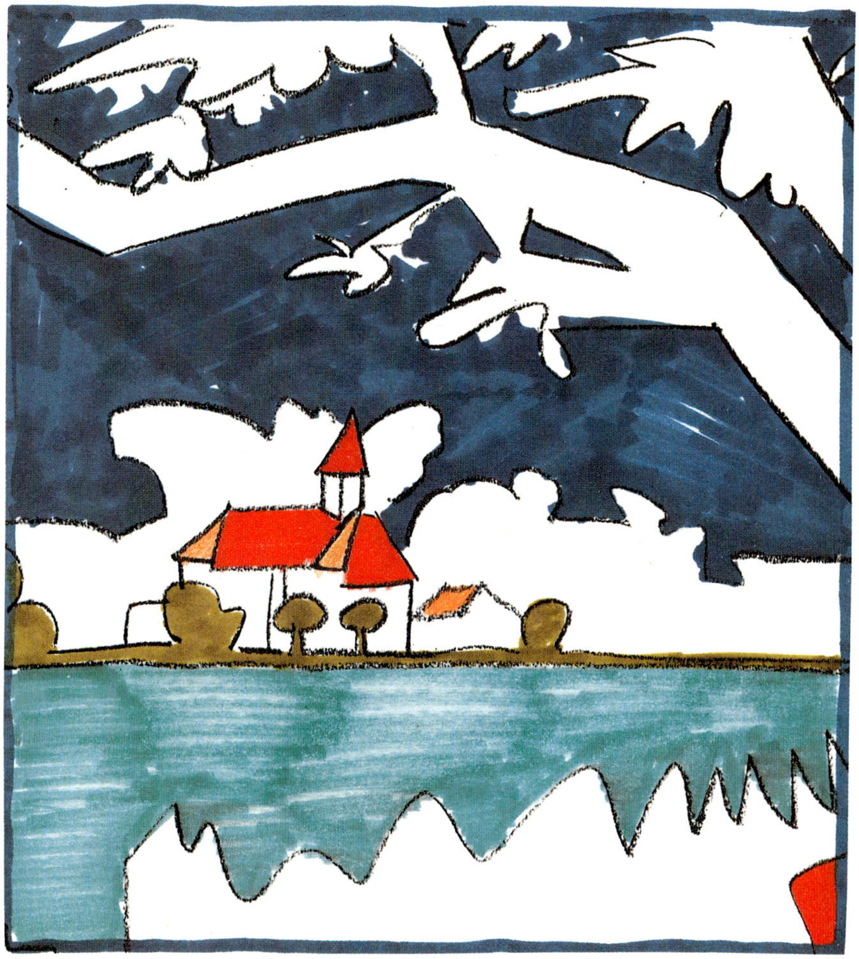

Concentrate on the shapes found in these two pictures, not what they represent. Turn the book upside-down to help you. The positive shapes are colored in the top picture; the negative ones, in the bottom picture. The artist intentionally chose colors that aren't found in nature in order to make it easier to see the shapes just as shapes.

Try this exercise with another picture (you can also use photographs). Focus on the shapes that form between objects, and try to draw only those shapes. You'll be amazed at how well you can draw the positive shapes by doing this.

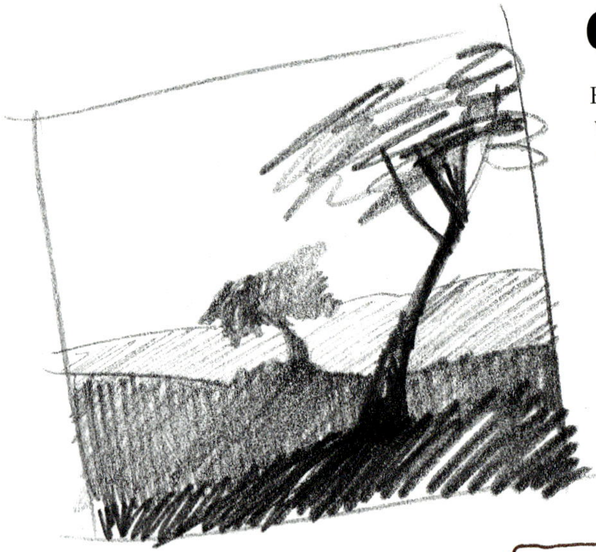

Composition

Every picture expresses something and provokes a certain reaction in the viewer. You either like a painting or you don't. A painting can seem happy or sad, aggressive or boring. Almost all artists want to express something through their paintings and convey to the observer what they are thinking or feeling. Color is vital to the expressiveness of a painting, but so is composition and perspective. Ultimately, every painting begins with the selection of the motif and the view—emphasizing what is most important to the artist.

In order to create the illusion of depth and three-dimensionality, we have to be familiar with the laws of perspective—the way in which things that are closer appear large and things that are farther away appear small. In landscape painting, an additional factor has to be taken into account—aerial perspective. Objects that are very distant from the observer appear not only smaller, but also lighter in color than objects that are nearer. The atmosphere between the object and the observer makes the object appear soft and distorted. The light grays in the sketch above give an impression of depth and distance. The same rules also apply to depicting height—there is a layer of air between the observer and the top of a tower. Thus, if you want to give the impression of height in a painting, make the upper areas lighter than the lower areas (right).

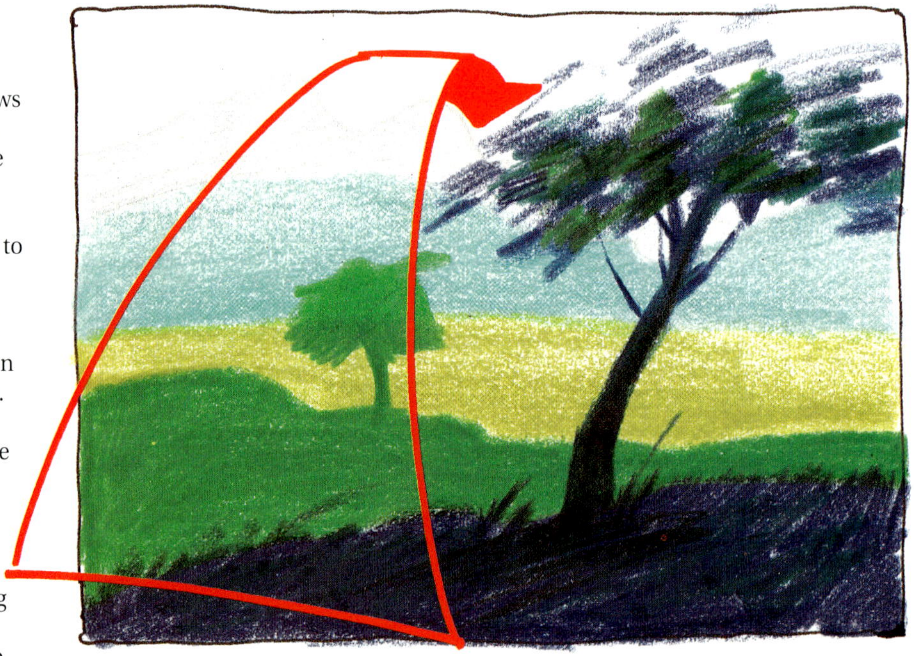

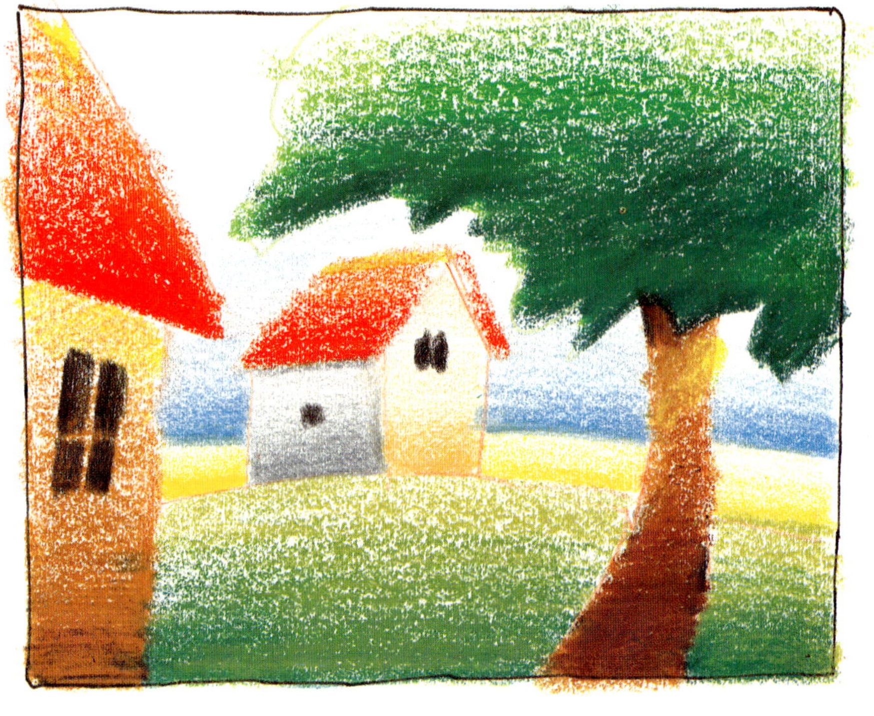

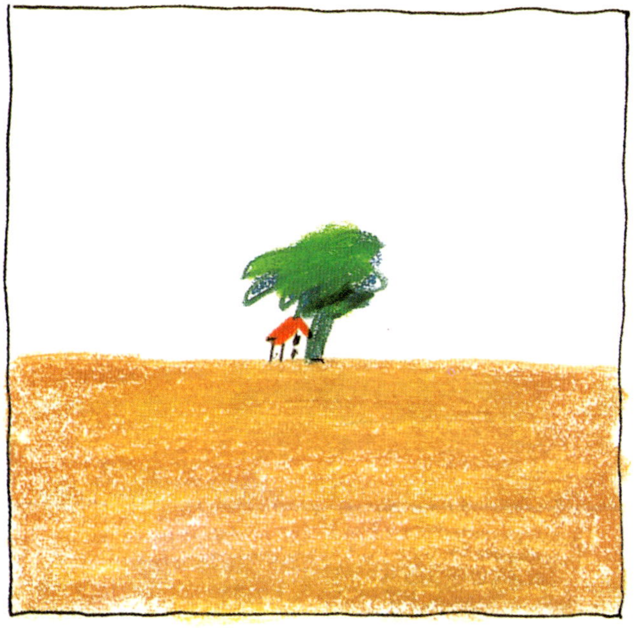

The composition can influence the expressiveness of a painting. A balanced or symmetrical composition, for example, gives the impression of tranquility. The tree here dwarfs the house, but it seems more protective than threatening because the house and the tree are surrounded by large, even areas of sky and ground which give a peaceful, harmonious impression. The sizes of the house and tree also make them seem very distant.

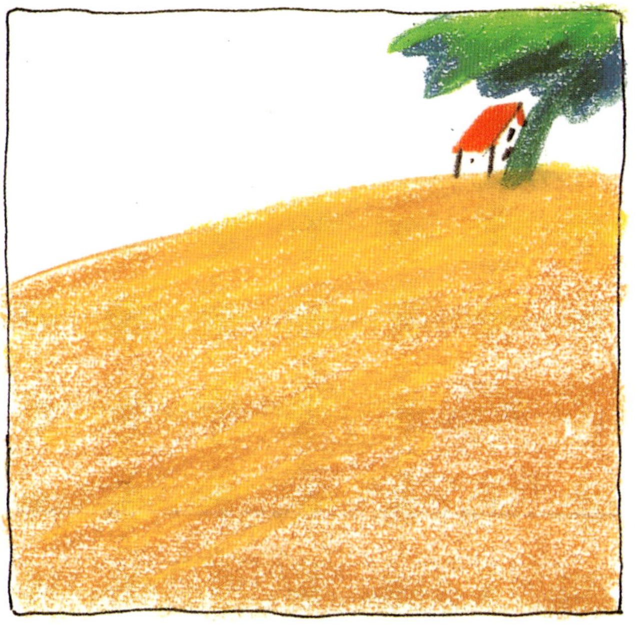

Simply changing the proportions and moving the house and the tree to an unusual location—for example, the upper right corner—creates tension in the composition. Anything that contradicts our sense of harmony and seems to "fall" out of the frame makes the observer take a second look, and thus creates tension. It can even go so far as to seem aggressive.

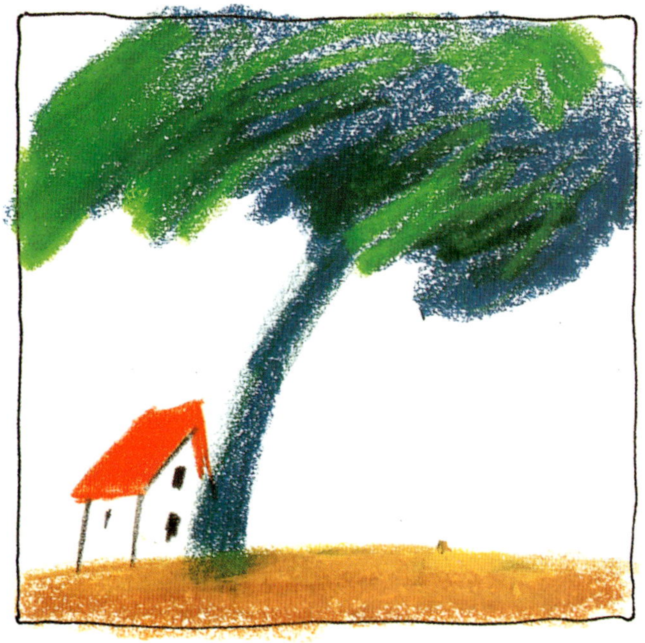

Large objects appear close. The tall tree is somewhat closer than the house but doesn't threaten it, since there is still "air" between the two. The slightly diagonal line of the tree brings movement to the composition, as diagonal lines are livelier than vertical or horizontal ones. Thanks to this movement, the house can also be slightly inclined without giving the impression that it's going to fall over.

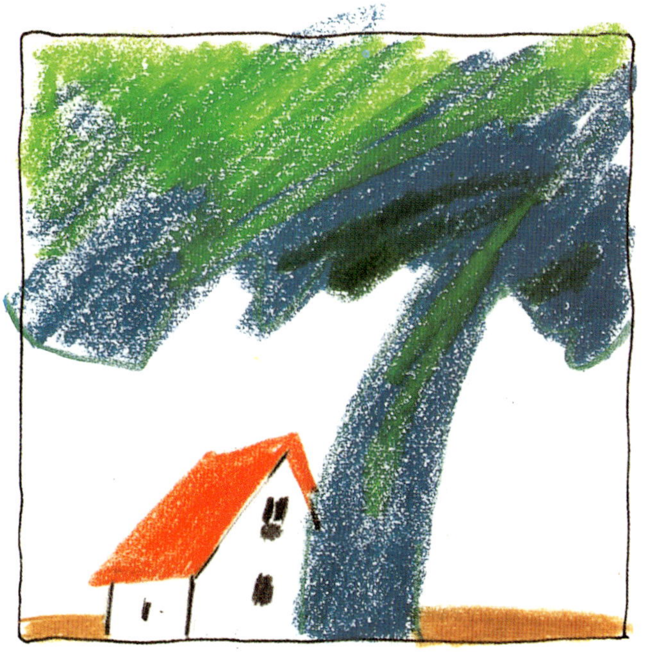

Objects that are cut off by the border can be an important means of expression, often creating a feeling of extreme closeness. They can even seem threatening or intimidating. Something that doesn't "fit in the frame" has to be important or unusual. The tree seems to threaten the smaller house, which seems a little closer because it too has been cut off.

Find a simple motif like this one and try to create different compositions and moods in quick sketches.

Working with Light and Shadow

A drawing that consists only of lines shows the motif, but it looks flat. Light and shadow give an object shape. Shadows, for example, transform a circle into a sphere.

For the sake of simplicity, let's stick with our tree example. If you draw it with just a line, the motif is recognizable, but it doesn't have any plasticity or depth. Yet if we imagine a light source from the upper right and sketch in the shadows, the tree becomes more three-dimensional and the trunk and top become round.

Generally speaking, we distinguish between two types of shadows: core shadows and cast shadows. The core shadow—that is, the shadow on an object itself—gives an object shape. The cast shadow, on the other hand, indicates the position of an object—whether it's standing, lying, or floating.

The core shadow is almost always lighter than the cast shadow, because it is illuminated by reflected light.

In landscape painting, the sun is the most significant light source. We cannot create shadows like we can with artificial light. The shape and length of the cast shadows depend entirely on the position of the sun. Since the sun moves in an arc around an object, the shadows can be short, like at midday, or long, like in late afternoon.

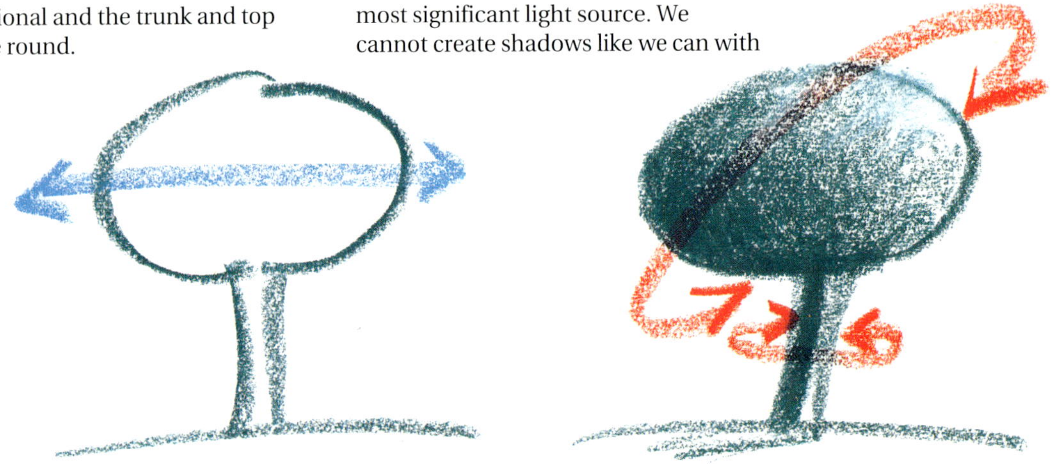

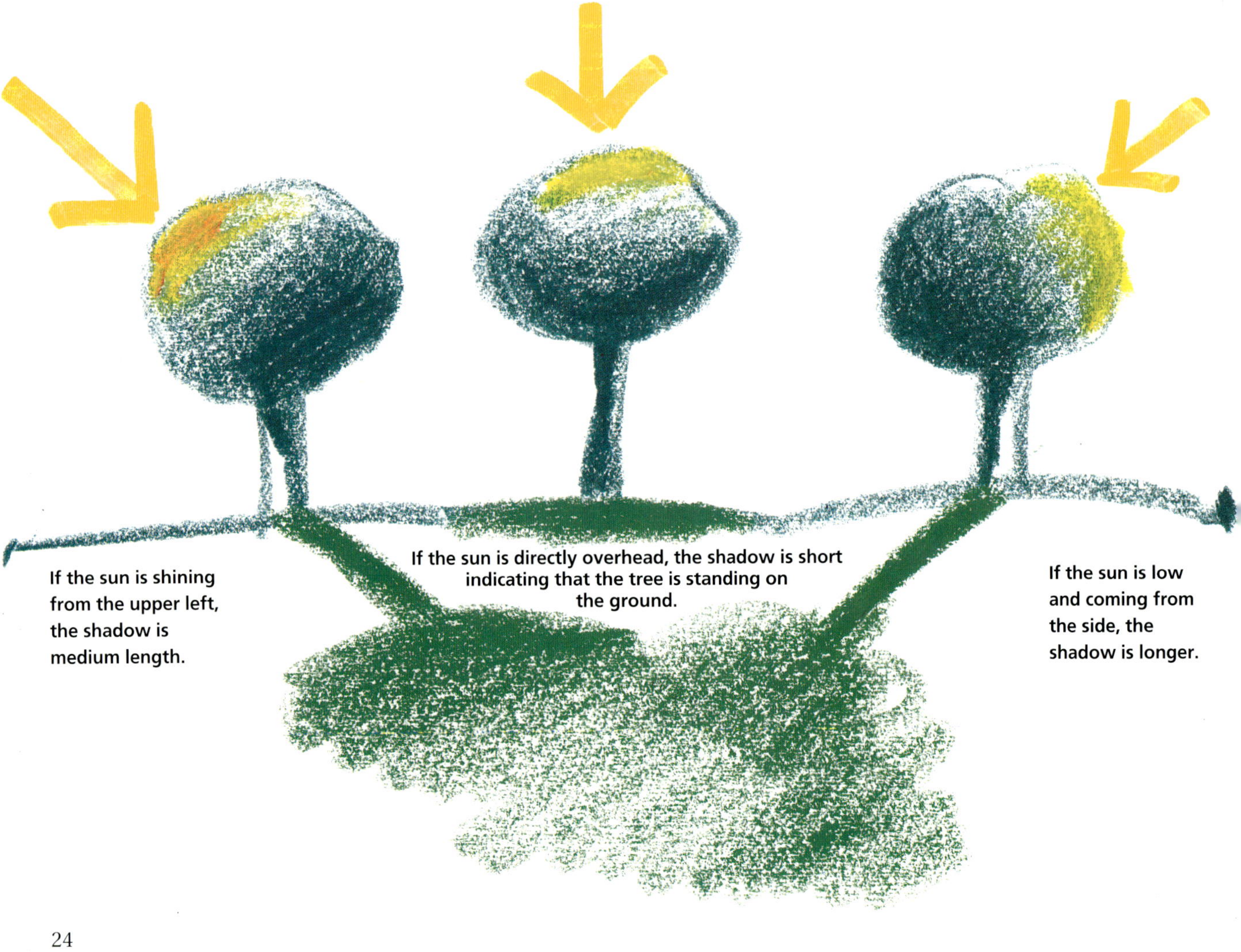

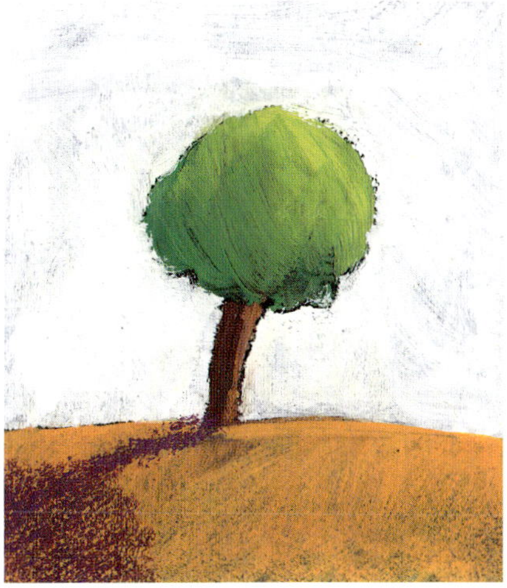

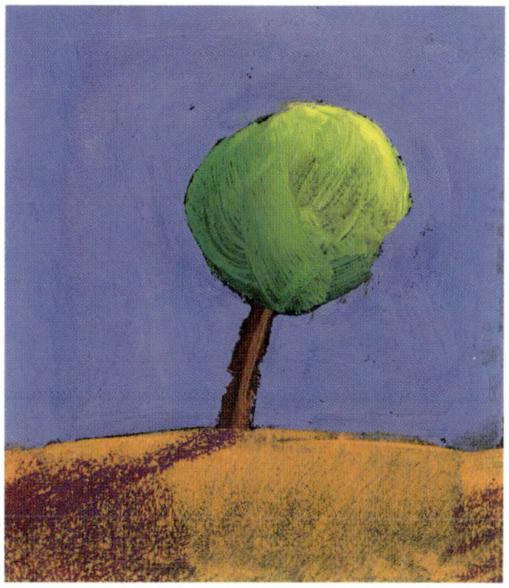

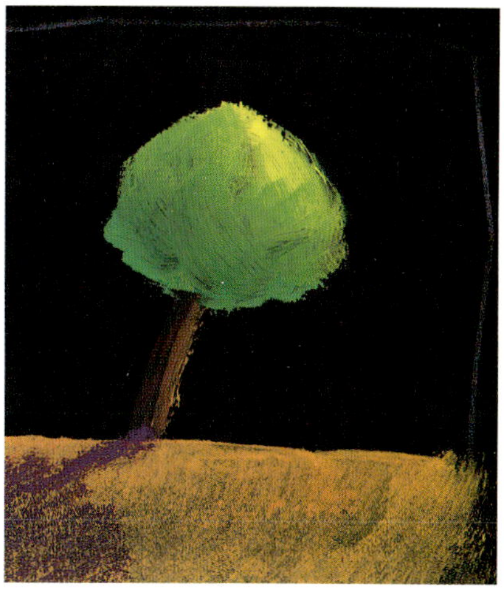

Shadows are influenced not only by light, but also by the colors of their surroundings. Look closely at the three pictures above. Are the tonal values of the tree, the core shadow, and the cast shadow equal in all three examples?

They are, in fact. When put against a light background, however, shadows appear darker, and vice versa. Even so, the cast shadow is darker than the core shadow.

Many people have trouble figuring out what colors to use for shadows. Unfortunately there are not any steadfast rules you can apply here. One thing is certain, though: Shadows are never simply black or gray because they reflect all kinds of other colors. Thus, shadows in nature frequently appear blue because they reflect the color of the sky. Even the yellow facade of a building or a red car can influence the color of a shadow. Of course, the color of the surface the shadow is on also plays a decisive role.

In order to illustrate this for you, many different colors were used for the shadows in the painting below. Notice how the light colors of the illuminated side of the tree were repeated, albeit somewhat darkened, in the dark side in order to liven it up.

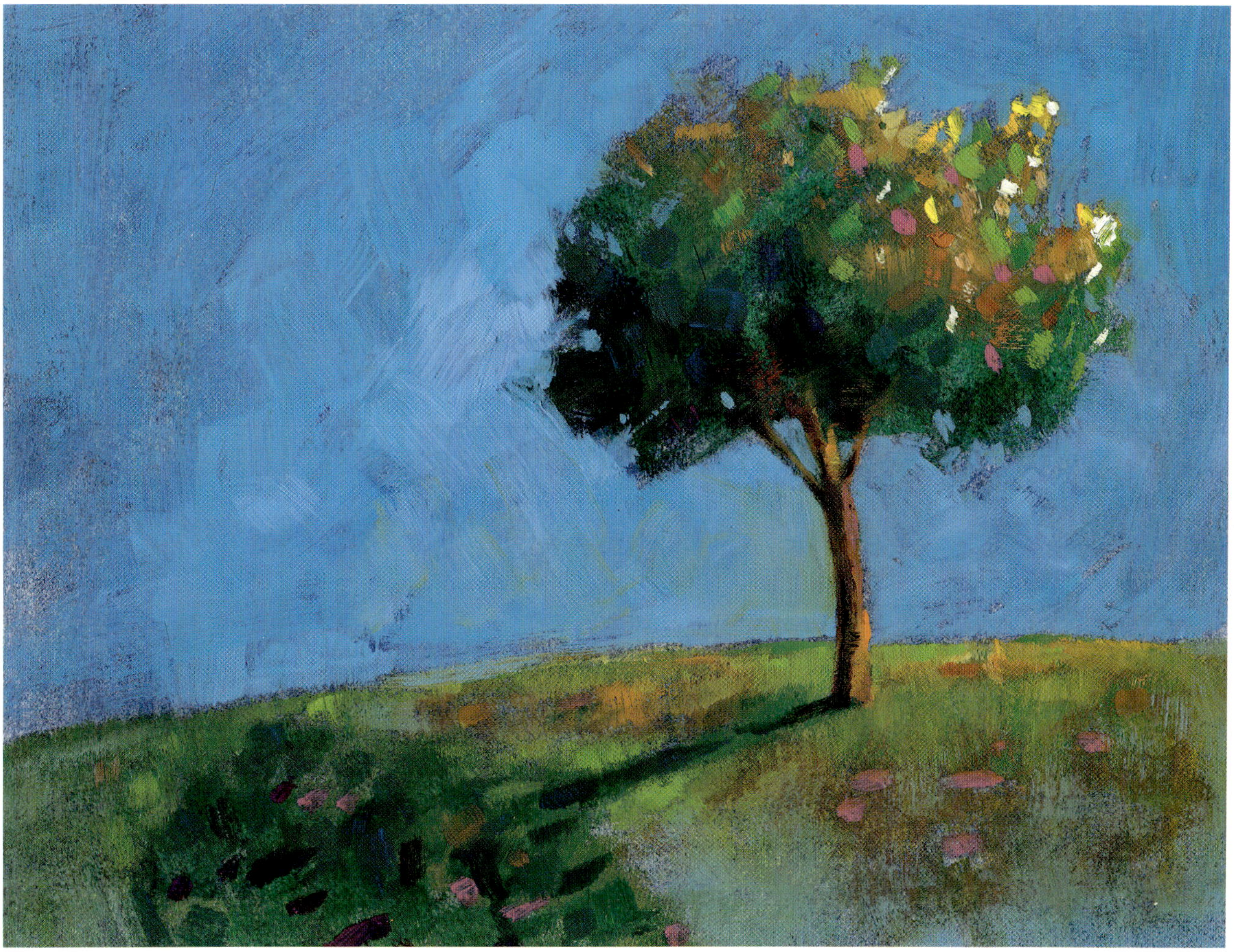

How Others Have Done It

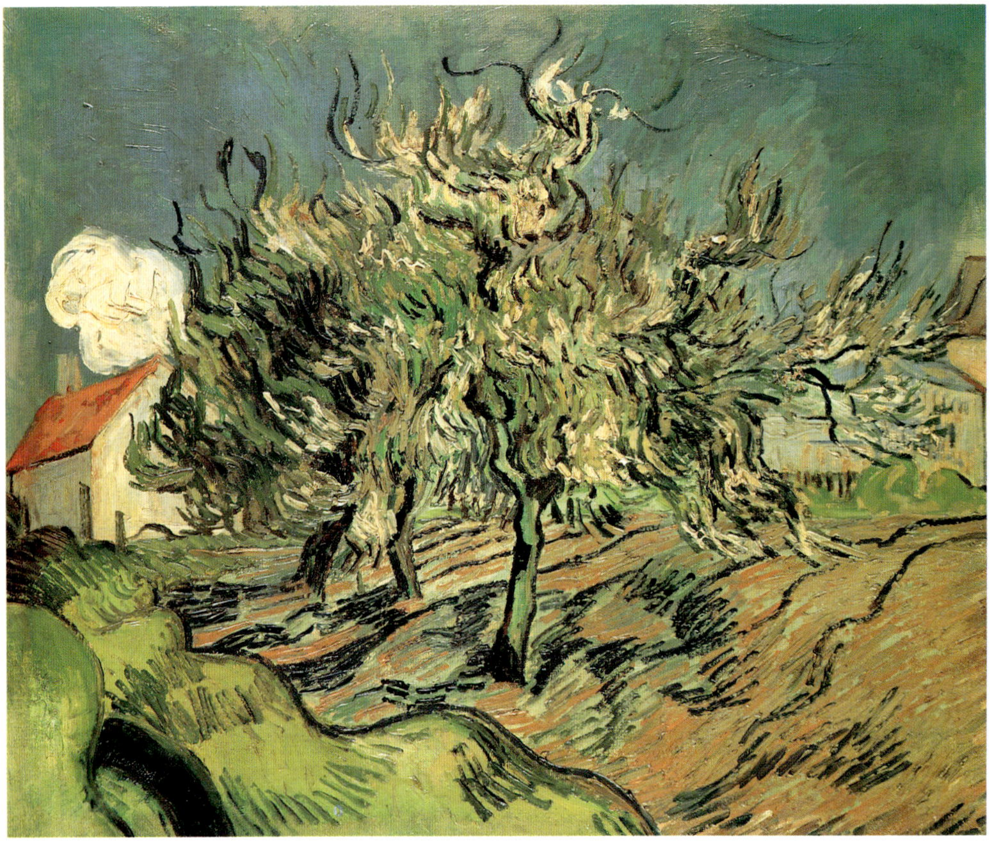

Vincent van Gogh
1853-1890

Vincent van Gogh,
Landscape with Three Trees and a House

Although the Dutch painter Vincent van Gogh sometimes had barely enough money to buy paints, he liked to apply them in thick coats, mixing them directly on the canvas. He worked quickly, sometimes not even waiting for the primer to dry. Van Gogh modeled his motif with his characteristic visible brush strokes, creating a feeling of movement even in tranquil compositions.

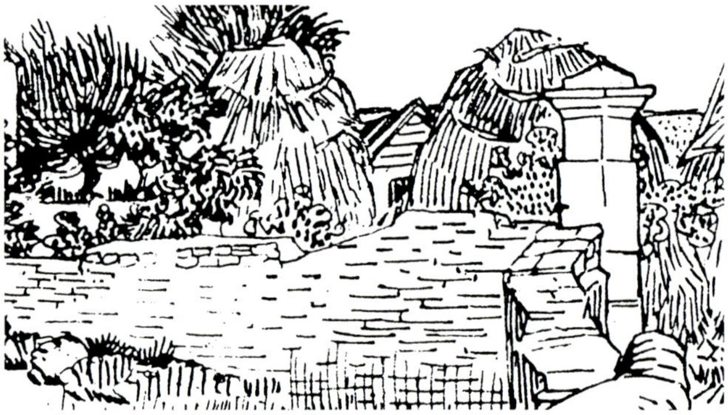

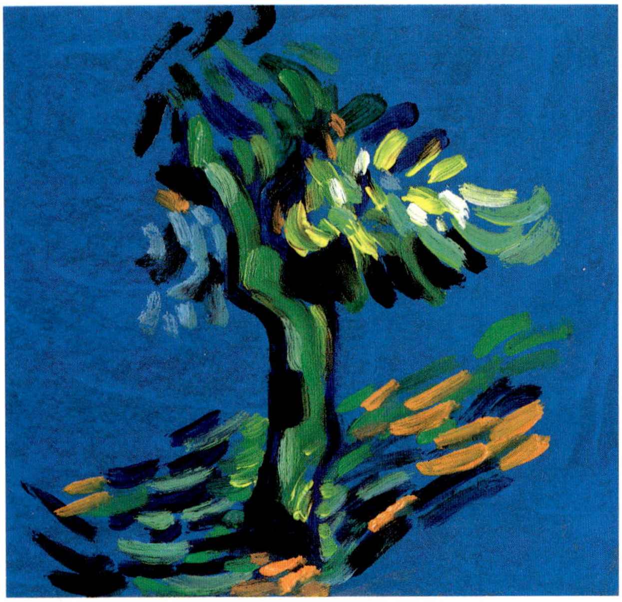

Van Gogh liked to work on a dark, often blue, background, which shimmered through subsequent layers of paint. In the study to the left you can see how the powerful blue accentuates the brilliance of the other colors. Many of van Gogh's paintings are actually painted drawings, and his drawings are drawn paintings. The way in which he formed objects using many small lines is particularly evident in his sketches. Look closely at the colors in the painting above. The meadow is not simply green and the sky is not simply blue; all the colors are repeated throughout the painting.

Pretend you are van Gogh: Transfer the drawing above to a painting, as was done with the study of the tree to the left. This will help you get a different feeling for colors and shapes.

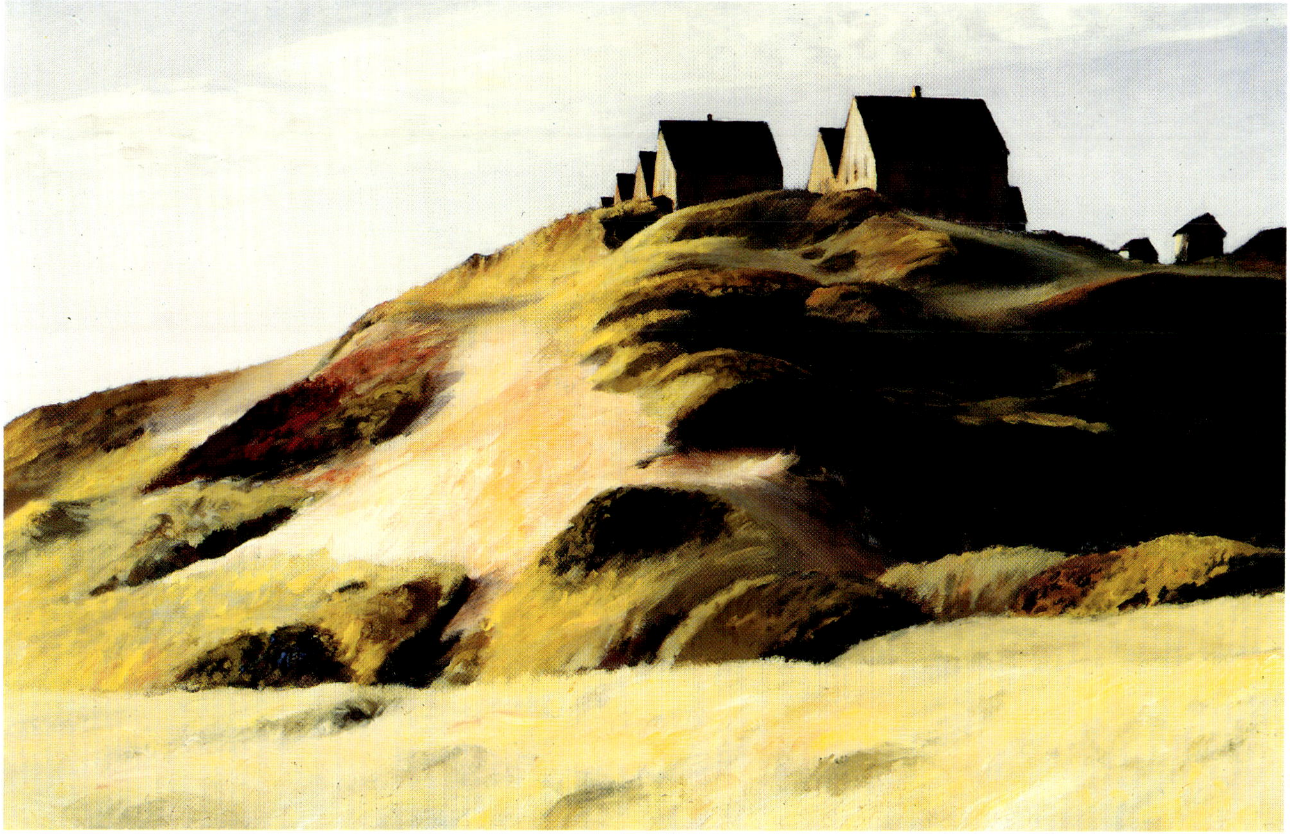

Edward Hopper, *Corn Hill, Truro, Cape Cod 1930*

The American artist Edward Hopper is known for his unusual compositions, which are simple but contain a definite rhythm. He tried to capture sunlight in his paintings—its effect on stark landscapes fascinated him. In later years, his favorite motifs came from Cape Cod. The painting entitled *Corn Hill* illustrates Hopper's fascination with the interplay of light and shadow. The composition consists of three horizontal sections: the foreground, the hills, and the sky. The light is coming from the left, throwing the hills deep into shadows.

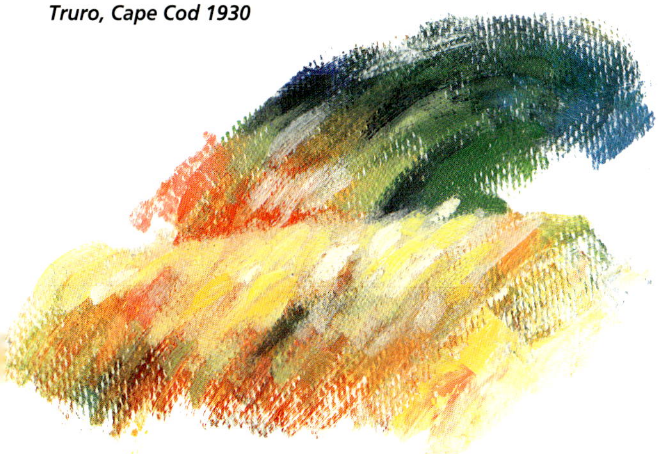

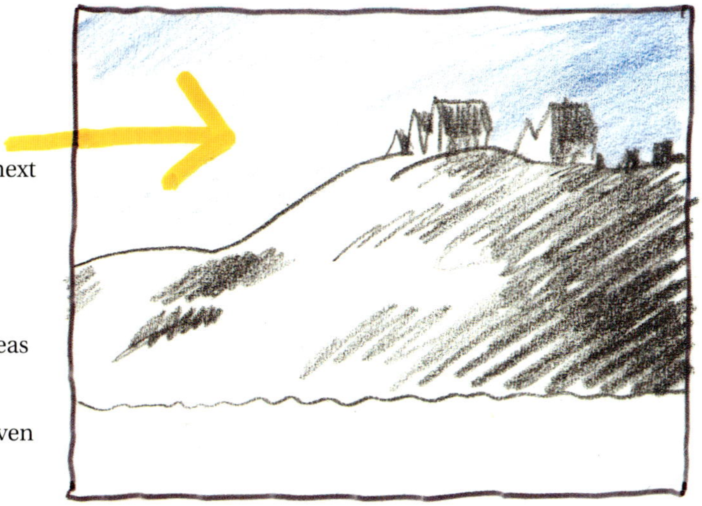

In contrast to van Gogh, who applied his brush strokes next to one another and barely waited for his paints to dry, Hopper was an extremely patient painter. He carefully worked out individual hues, created nuances by continuously painting over areas, and always allowed background colors to shimmer through. The example above is an attempt to illustrate Hopper's technique. Areas that at first glance appear to consist of one color are actually made up of many different colors.

Most of the colors in Hopper's landscapes are cool. Even the sunlight isn't particularly warm.

John Constable
1776-1837

The English painter John Constable is often called the father of Expressionism. He preferred landscape motifs, creating unusual and expressive compositions. He also liked to paint and draw outside as much as he could, especially in the summer. In his studio in Hampstead, he assembled the individual sheets he had used outside into a huge sketch in preparation for his large paintings. His expressive nature sketches are extremely freeform and impressionistic. He wasn't afraid to apply the paints with a knife or with his finger. He used a brown or red background for many of his landscape studies; he used a lighter, pinkish gray background for his seascapes.

The two details below show the spontaneous brush strokes used in the painting. Despite this, however, each little spot was carefully planned and meticulously applied.

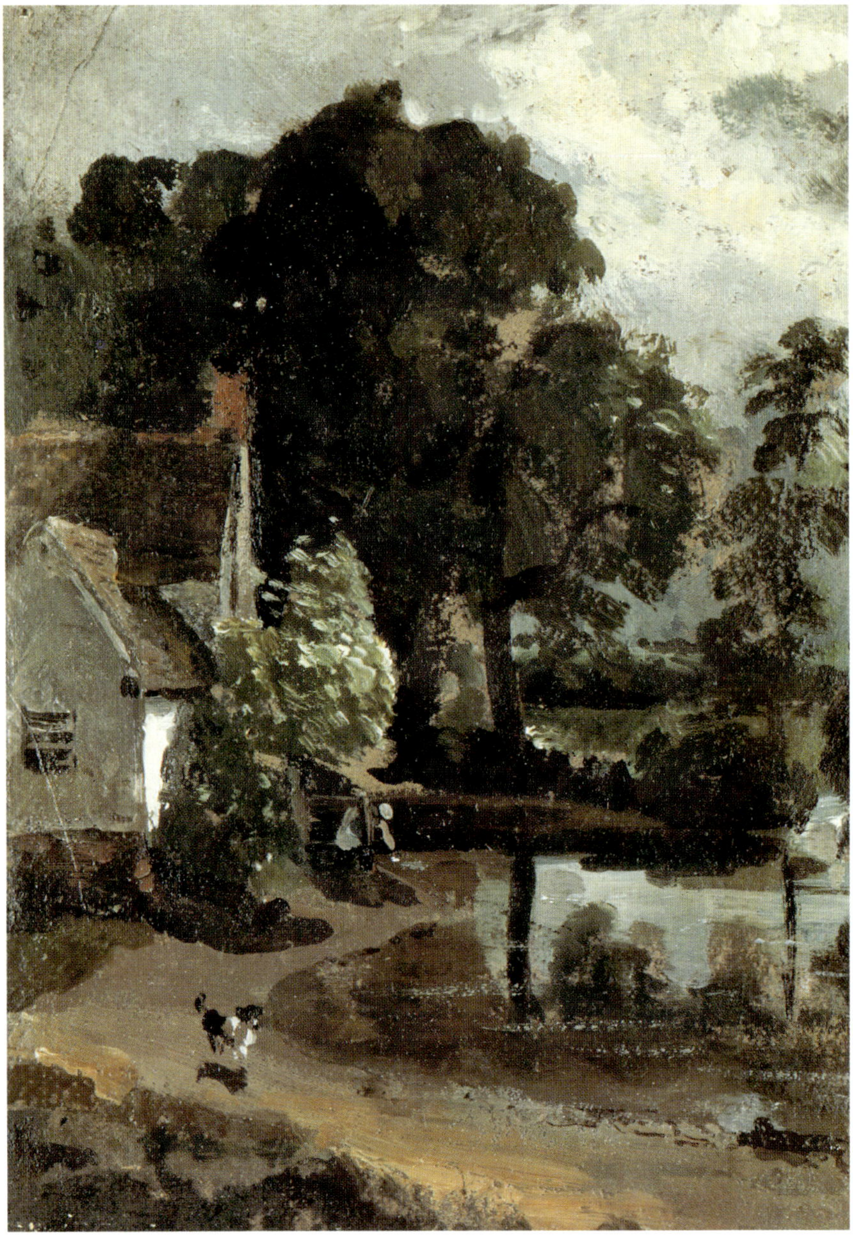

John Constable,
Willy Lott's House

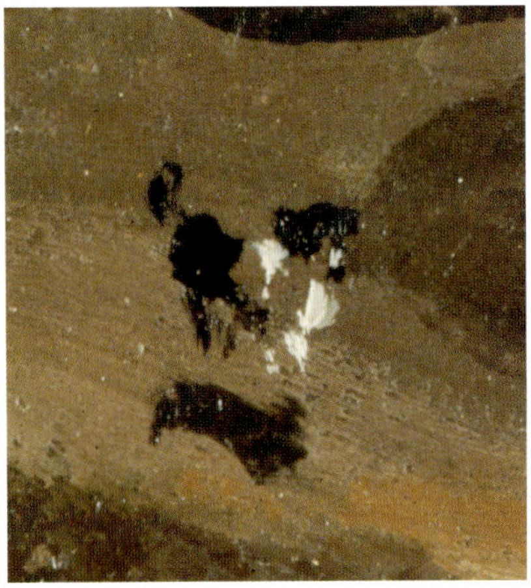

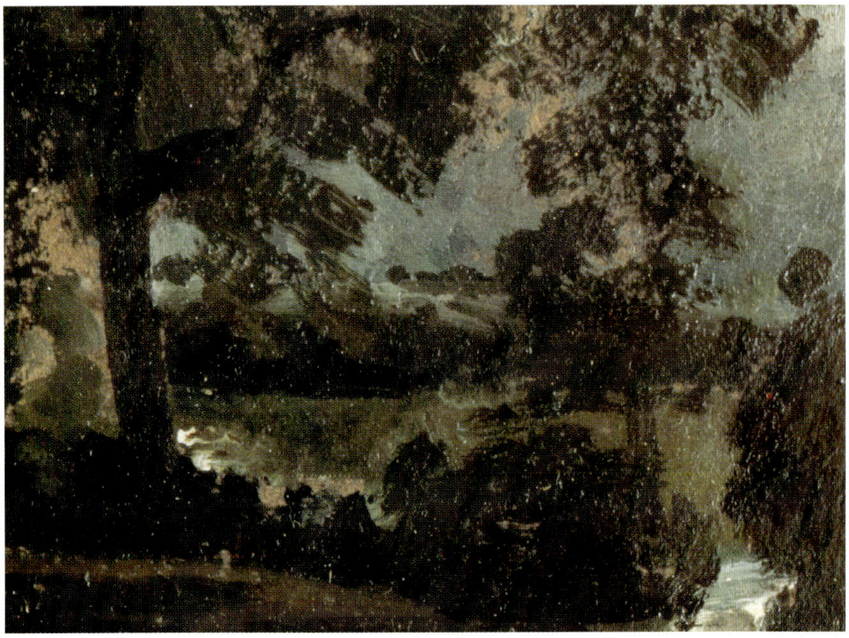

The little dog provides an excellent example of Constable's precise brushwork. If you look at it out of context, it seems almost abstract. Constable painted it using approximately ten black brush strokes and five white brush strokes, applying them with absolute precision. This precision is also evident in the person by the house and in all the other details. The dark colors were applied on top of the lighter ones with a soft brush. The direct brushwork is reminiscent of the elegance of Chinese paintings.

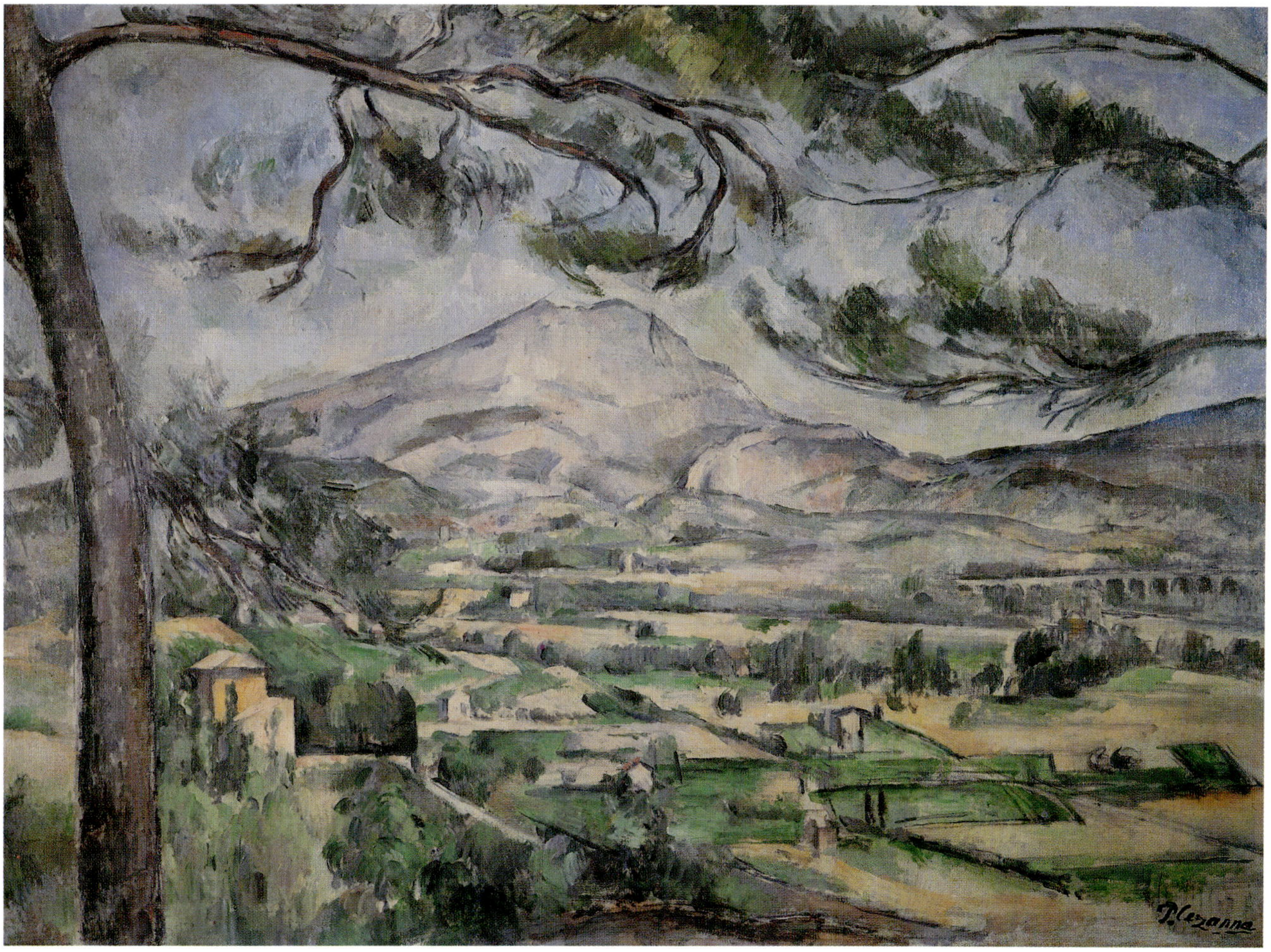

Paul Cézanne, *La Montagne Sainte-Victoire*

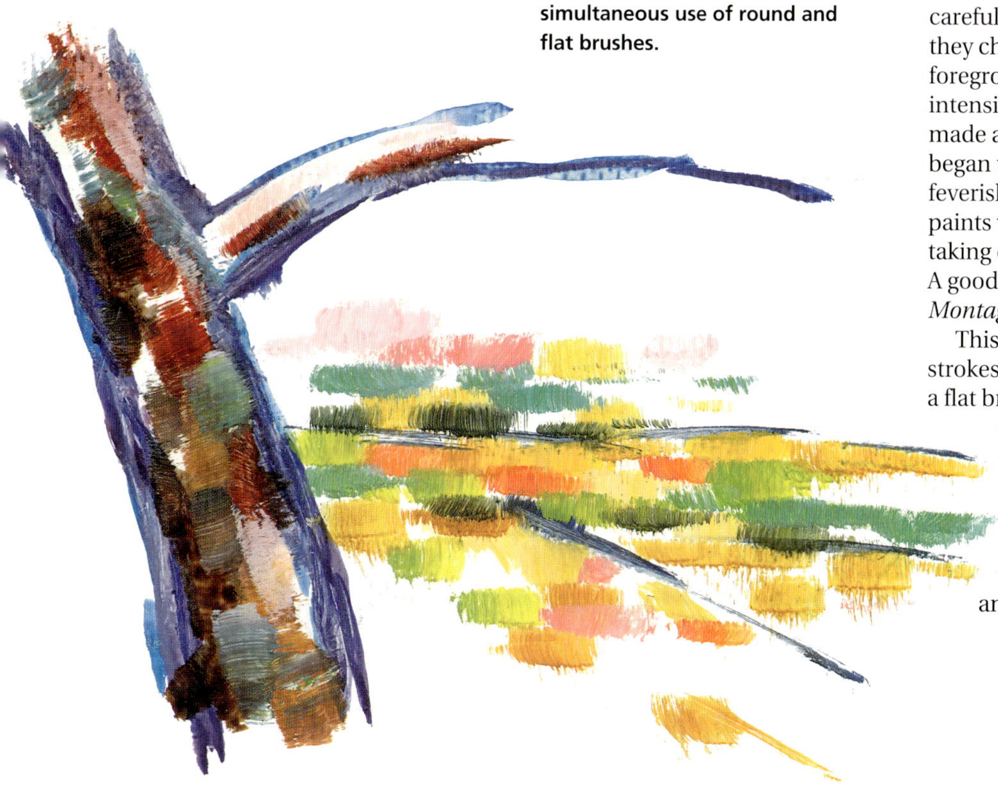

Cézanne was a master of the simultaneous use of round and flat brushes.

Paul Cézanne studied his motifs carefully, analyzing colors and how they change, the background and the foreground, depth and the varying intensity of the colors. Once he had made all the important decisions, he began to work quickly, almost feverishly. He rubbed and worked the paints with his brush, each stroke taking on a shape and color all its own. A good example of this technique is *La Montagne Sainte-Victoire.*

This composition is full of layered strokes, which Cézanne applied with a flat brush. The contours of the mountains and the shapes of the tree, on the other hand, were applied with a pointed brush and many layers of ultramarine blue. Cézanne was very conscious of the shapes and contours in his compositions.

Sketches

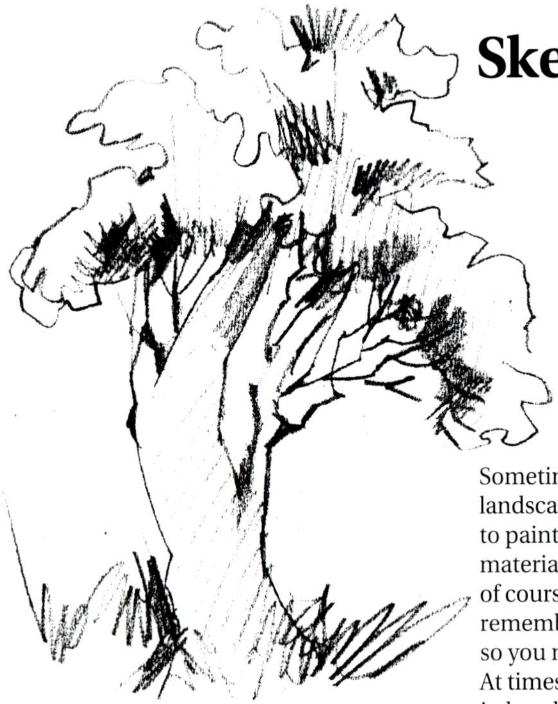

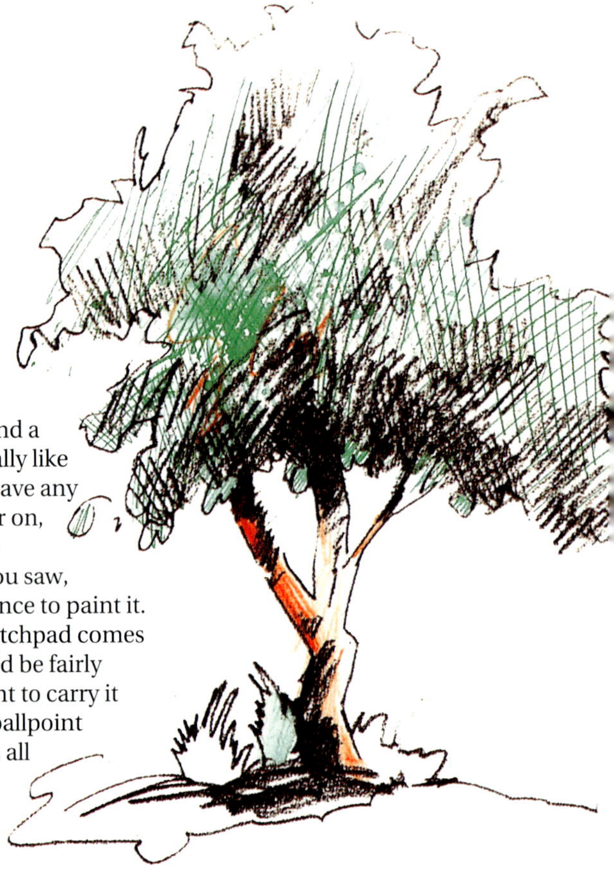

Sometimes you might find a landscape that you'd really like to paint, but you don't have any materials with you. Later on, of course, it's difficult to remember everything you saw, so you never get the chance to paint it. At times like these, a sketchpad comes in handy. The pad should be fairly small because you'll want to carry it with you, and a pencil, ballpoint pen, or felt-tip marker is all that's needed to make a note of a thought or an impression.

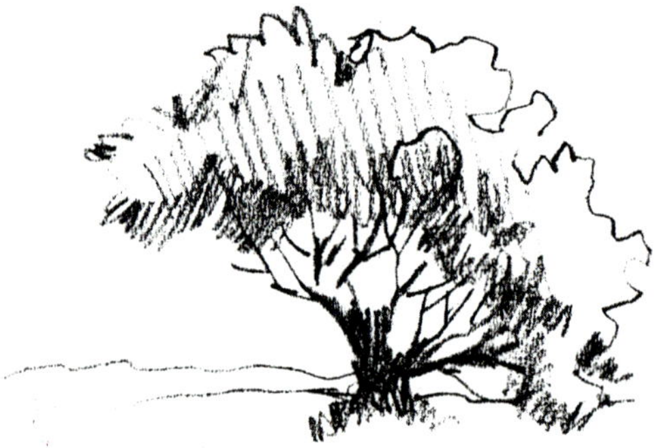

Just what is a sketch? Generally speaking, a sketch is used to quickly capture something you don't want to forget. It can be an idea, a motif that pops into your head, or even the preliminary composition for a painting. Sketches can be invaluable in helping you remember what you've seen, particularly on vacations or trips. They are also useful for studying the shape and nature of an object. The artist here was very interested in trees and bouquets. Shapes, colors, and tonal values were sketched constantly during the different seasons. In this way, the artist was able to become very familiar with these plants and now can add them to scenes where they don't actually exist.

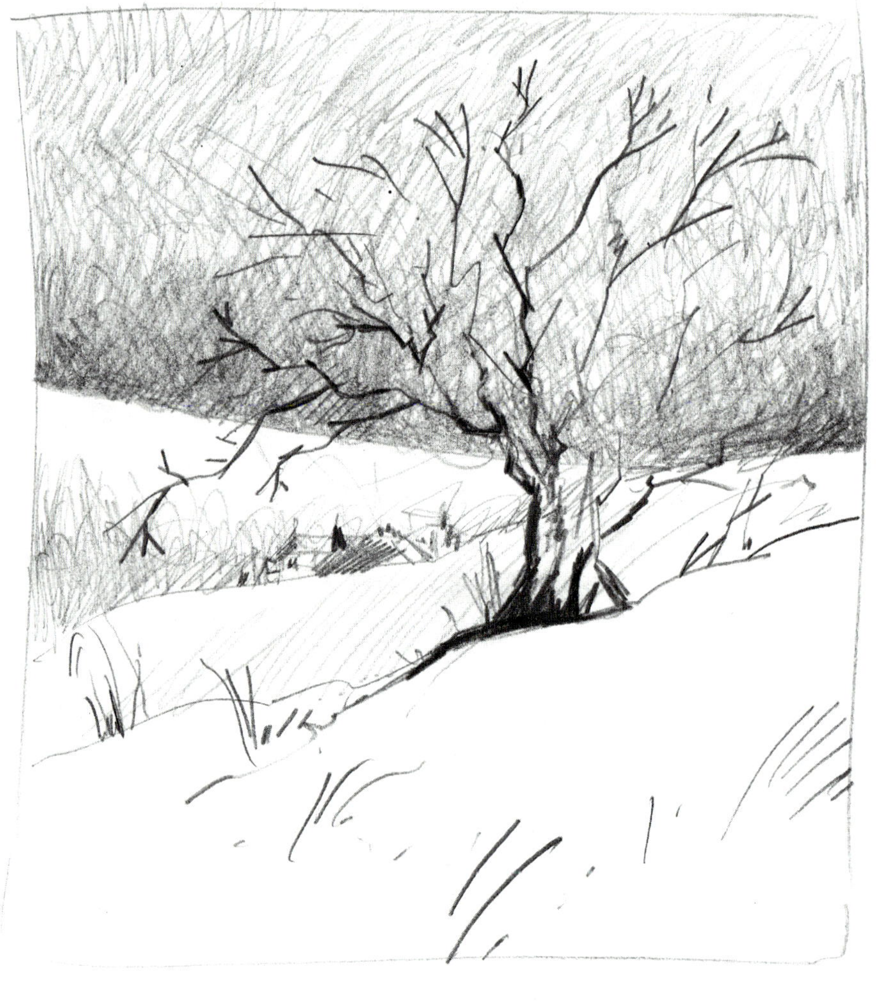

When you are on a trip, you can use your sketchpad as a sort of diary. Sketches are even more personal than a photo album, because you're capturing your own feelings and moods.

If you get in the habit of carrying your sketchpad everywhere, you'll soon have a large supply of ideas and motifs that you can refer back to any time you need inspiration. The paper you use for sketching is unimportant. The most practical setup is a pad that has a cover to protect your sketches, but you can also use a notebook or a bound book with blank pages. The latter has the advantage that it provides a solid surface for drawing, so you can lay it on your lap if needed.

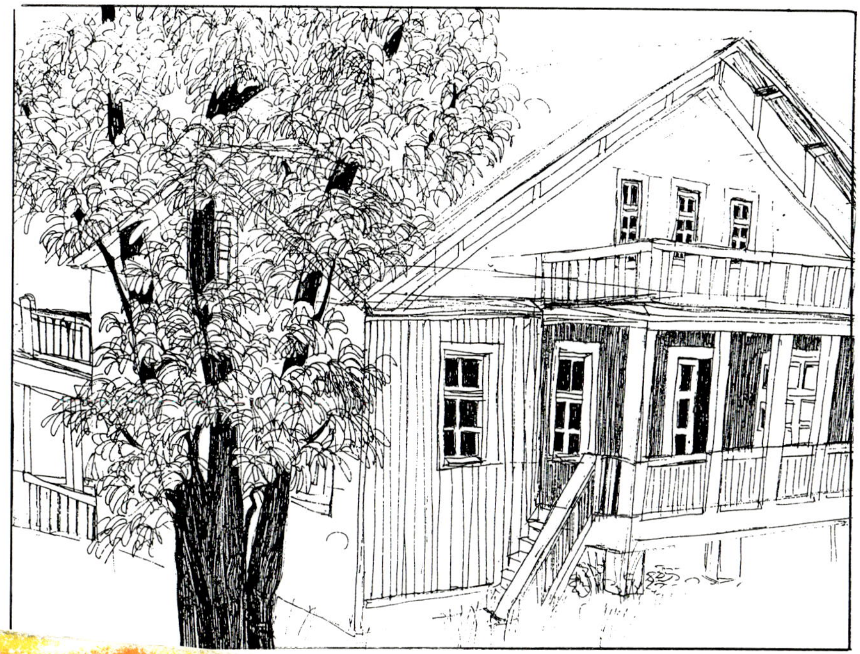

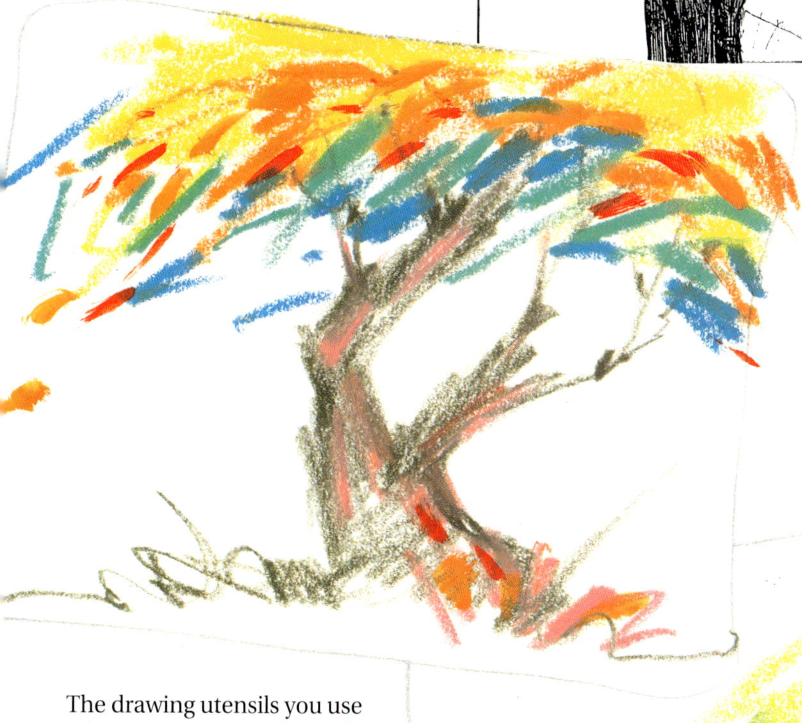

On the opposite page, you can see a number of sketches done on the theme of "trees." The sketch directly above shows a wooden house and a detailed tree sketched in Finland. To the left and below are quick sketches made using colored chalks. In the sketch below, the primary concern was with the interplay between positive and negative space.

The drawing utensils you use are also up to you. Pencils work just as well as ballpoint pens or felt-tip markers. Colored pencils and chalks are more difficult to manage, but the advantage is that you can work in color. Chalks are particularly delicate, since they break and smear easily. In any case, be sure to take a sketchpad along on your next vacation. You'll be surprised at how quickly your drawings improve and how much you enjoy your sketches when you return home.

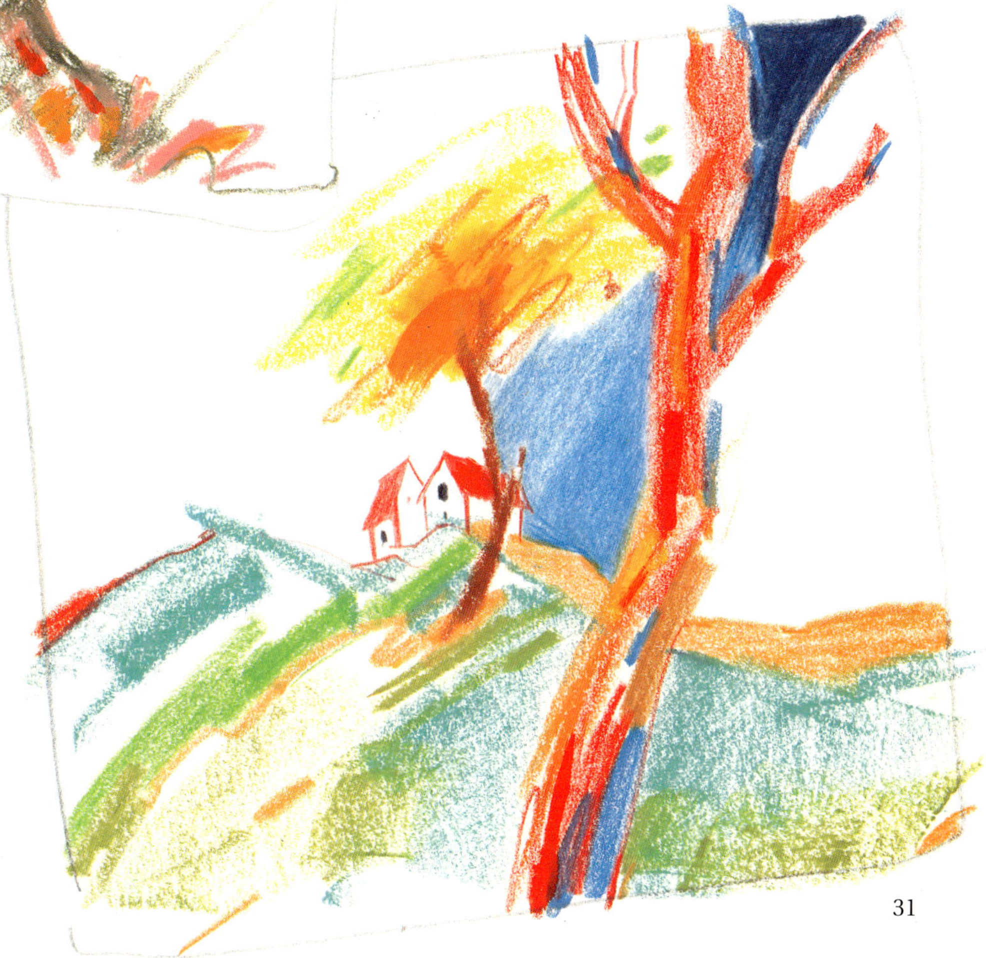

Painting a Landscape and Houses

with Brian Bagnall

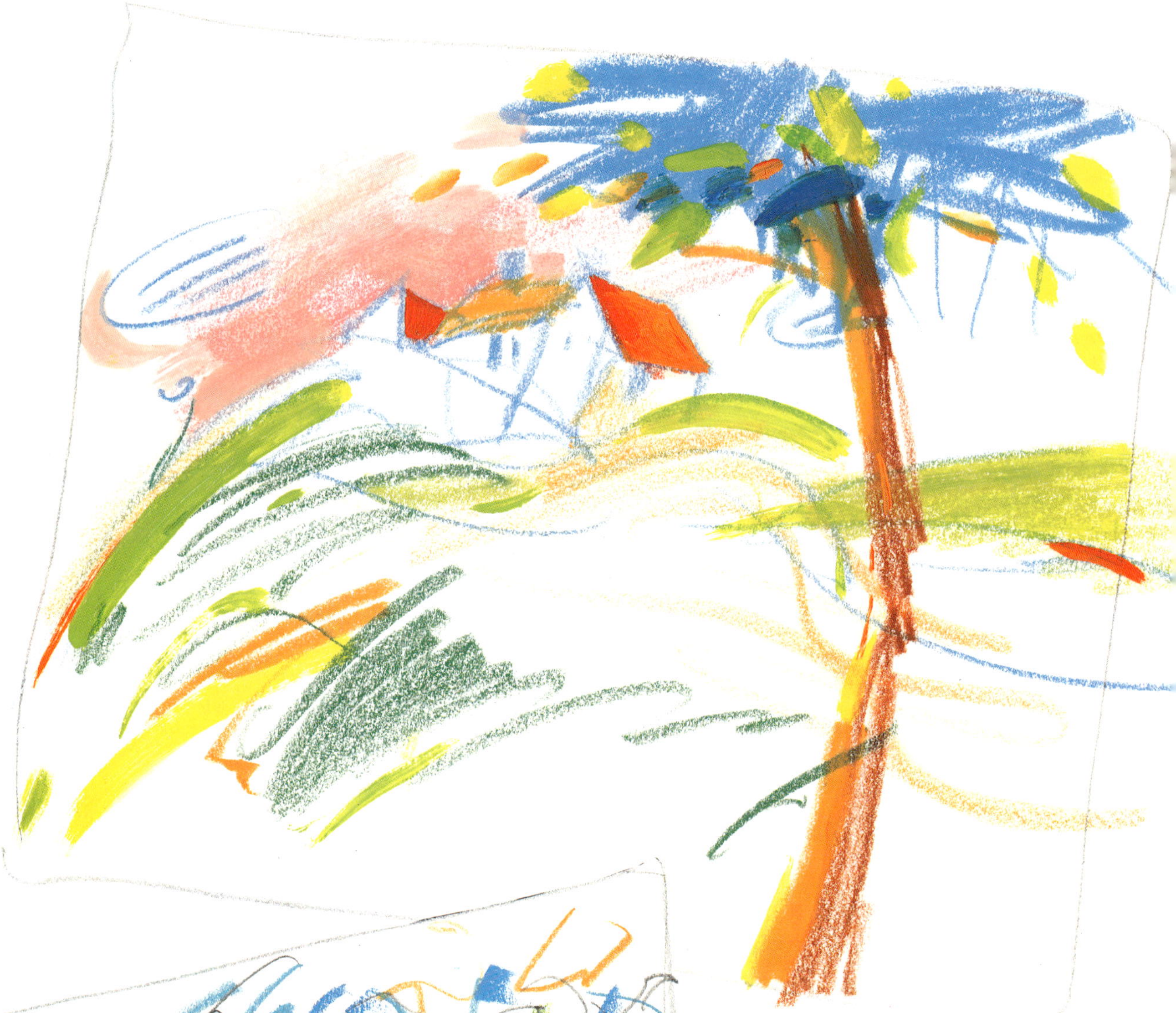

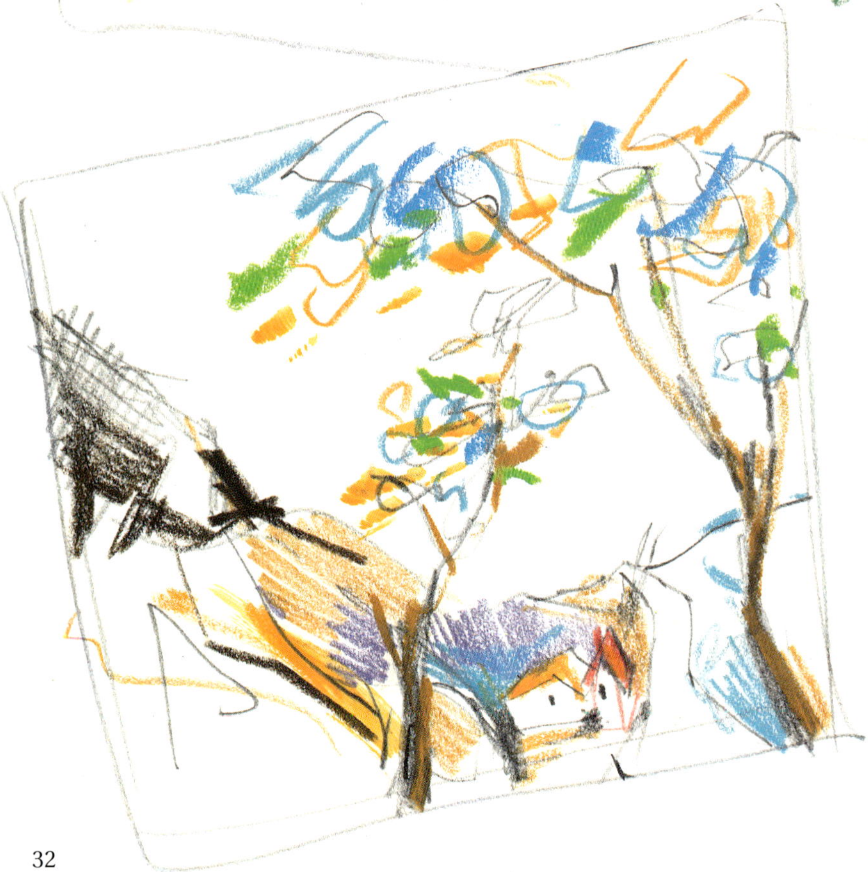

Let's stay with the topic of sketches for a minute. On these pages you can see how they can be used in actual practice. When I decided on the motif of "a landscape and houses," I immediately grabbed my sketchpad and began leafing through it. After I had selected a couple of suitable sketches, I added color to some of them (others were already in color). I wanted to paint a simple landscape, and I liked the idea of associating man-made architecture with the natural static of plants and trees.

Making use of the sketchpad: I got the idea for my oil painting by combining several sketches from my sketchpad. Color sketches help determine what mood the painting should express.

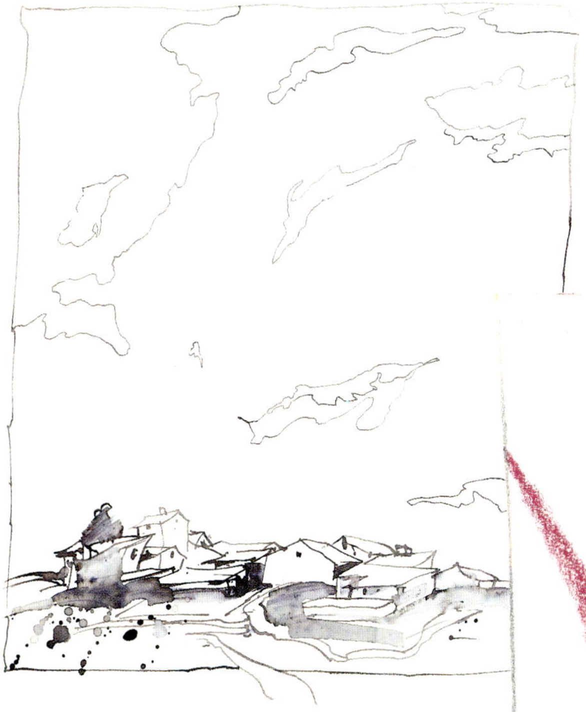

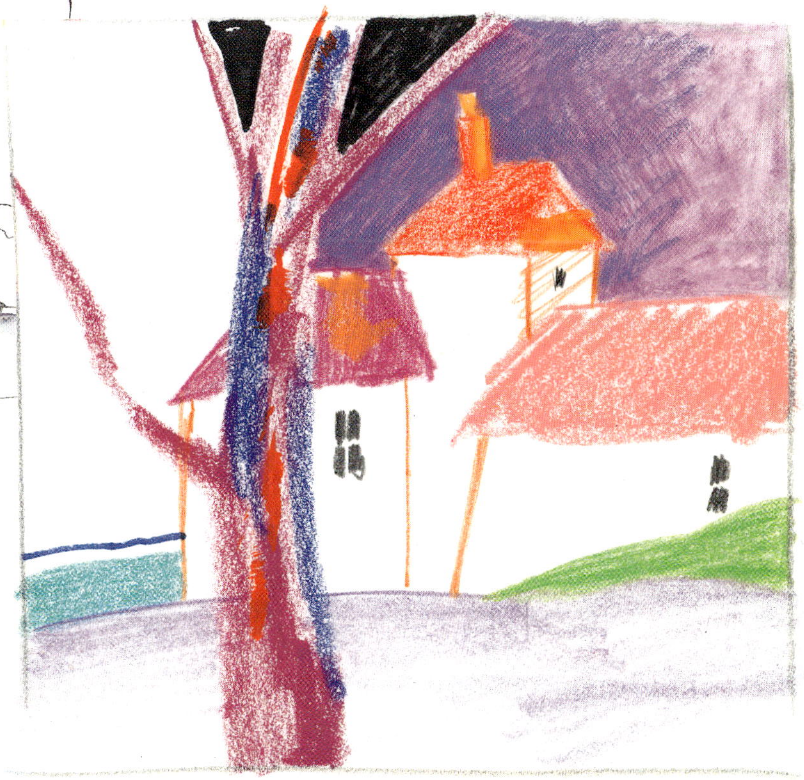

You usually won't be able to paint the beautiful view or unusual landscape you see before you as is—you will have to create your own composition out of it. In other words, you must decide which elements are important for the painting and which ones can be left out. In the sketches on the opposite page, the trees dominate the composition; in the sketch above, the sky dominates. I decided to leave the tree in the foreground and make the houses more prominent. I also incorporated the negative space between the tree and the sky as an equal element in the composition. After I made the chalk sketch (above right), I made one on colored cardboard using oils, allowing the black to show through the paints. I then used this sketch as the model for my painting.

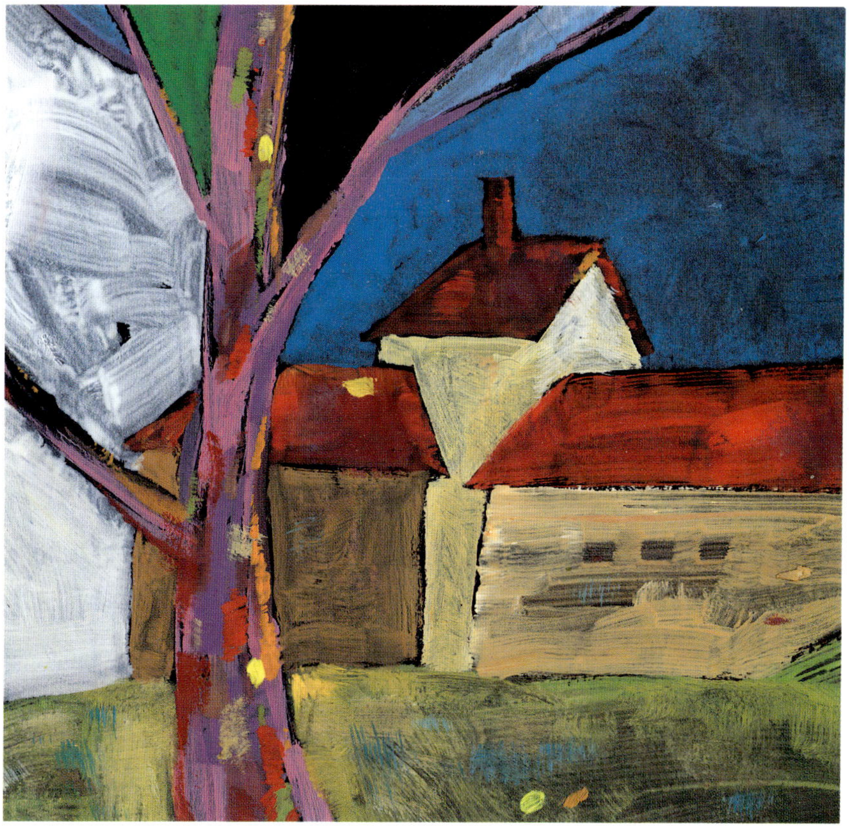

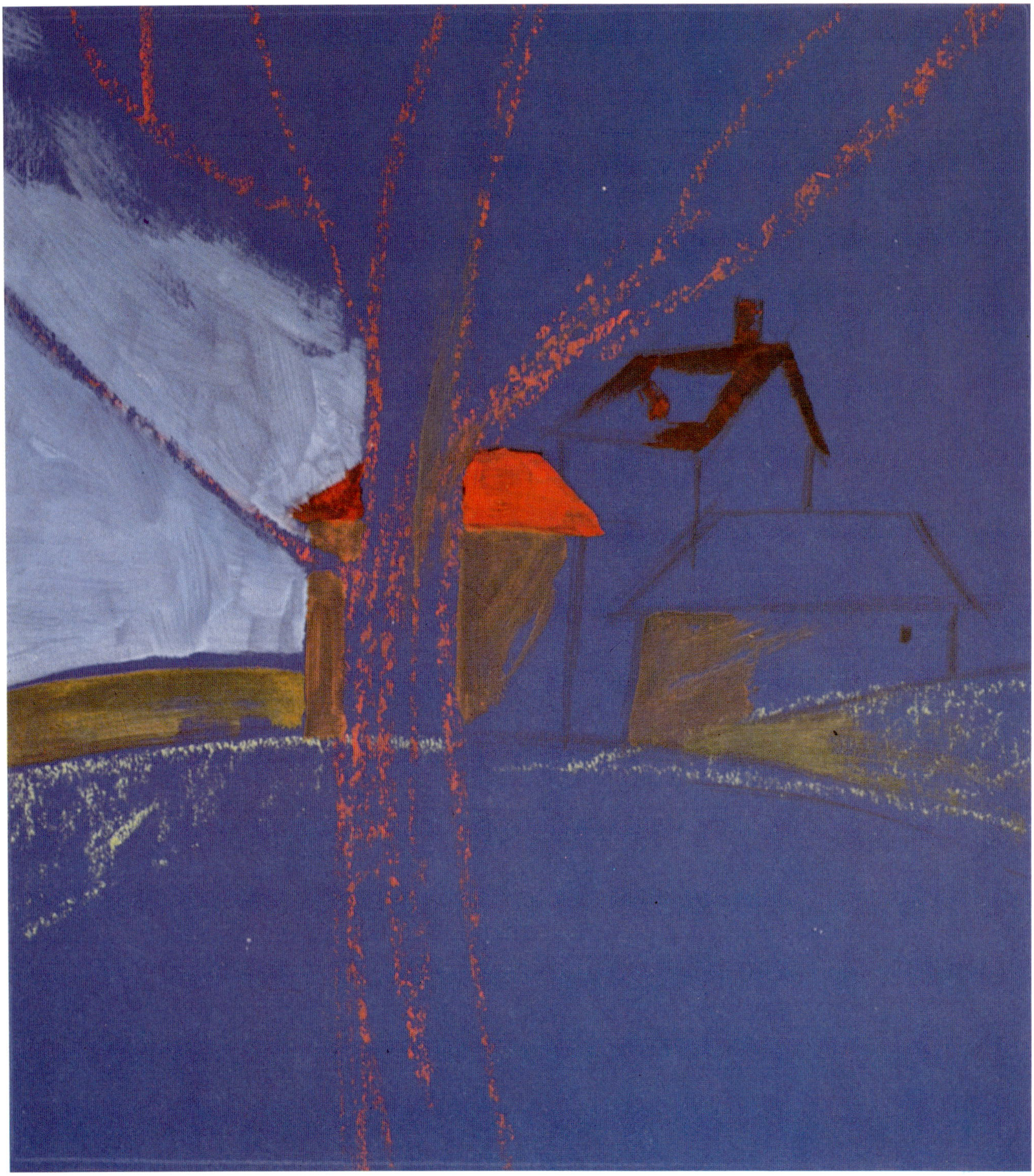

After I had analyzed my sketches more closely, I changed the composition somewhat. I gave the houses more "air" and replaced the black background with dark blue. A dark background makes the other colors livelier, more brilliant. I drew in the preliminary lines in red and light green pastels. At this stage, I prefer to work with pastels rather than with charcoal, since pastels are not as prone to smearing. Once I was satisfied with the composition, I began to "rough out" simple shapes. I worked on several different areas of the painting at the same time in order to get a feel for the entire composition and so as not to focus too much on details at the beginning—particularly because I already knew how I wanted my final painting to look. By the way, it's all right if the pastels show through later.

Colors used:

titanium white, cadmium red light, lemon yellow, cadmium orange, cadmium yellow, alizarin crimson, burnt umber, yellow ochre, chromium oxide green, violet, fuchsia, ultramarine blue

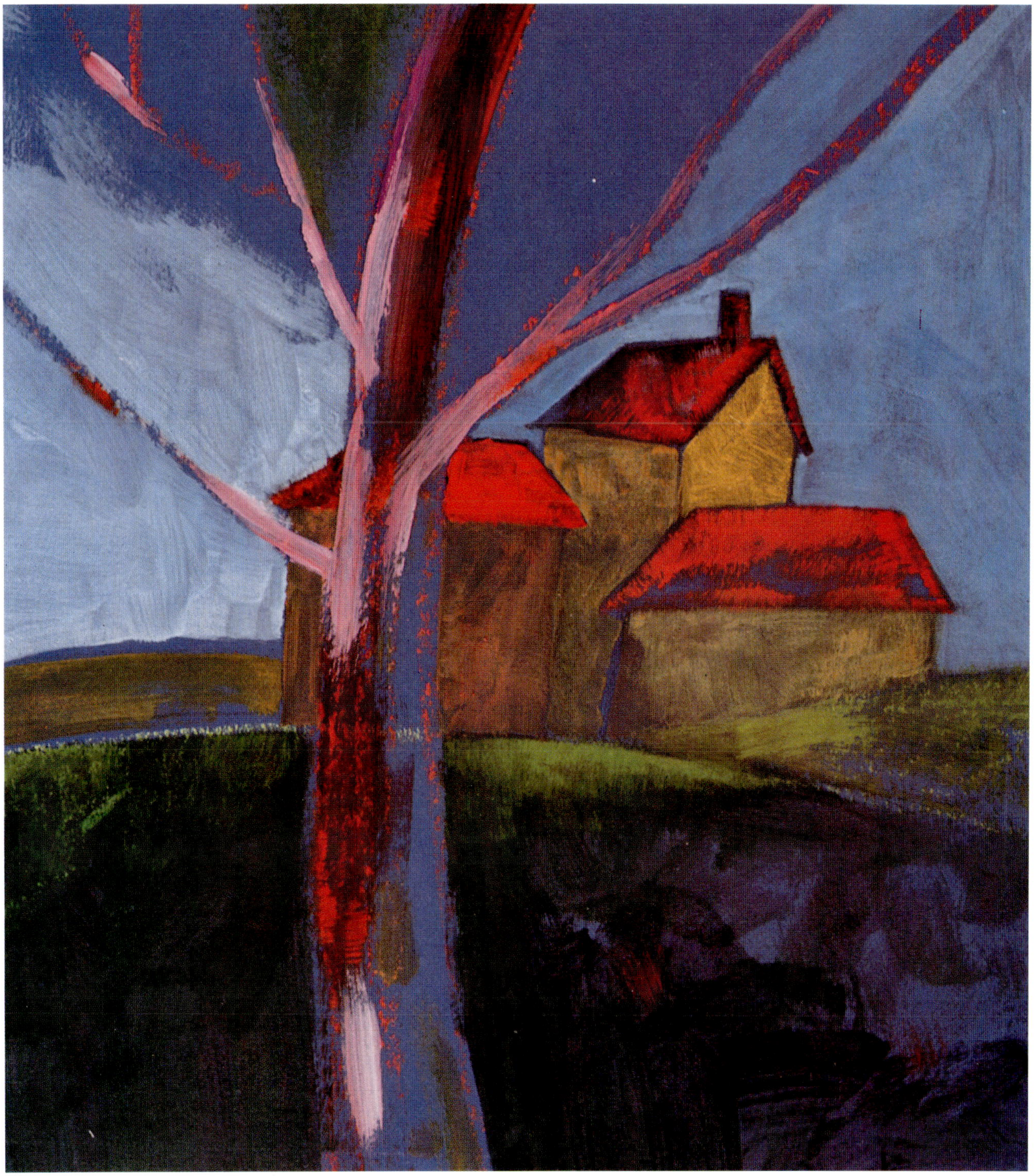

Next, I modeled all the areas that are important for the composition. This was accomplished by carefully planning the color scheme and concentrating on each area. Notice that the shapes between the branches (negative space) play just as important a role as the rooftops and the meadow. This interplay creates an interesting rhythm of shapes and colors. I gradually began to build up the walls of the houses, and I applied highlights to the trunk of the tree and the edge of the meadow. The intense blue of the background is an important element in the picture and is incorporated into all the other objects, either as a contrast or as a highlight.

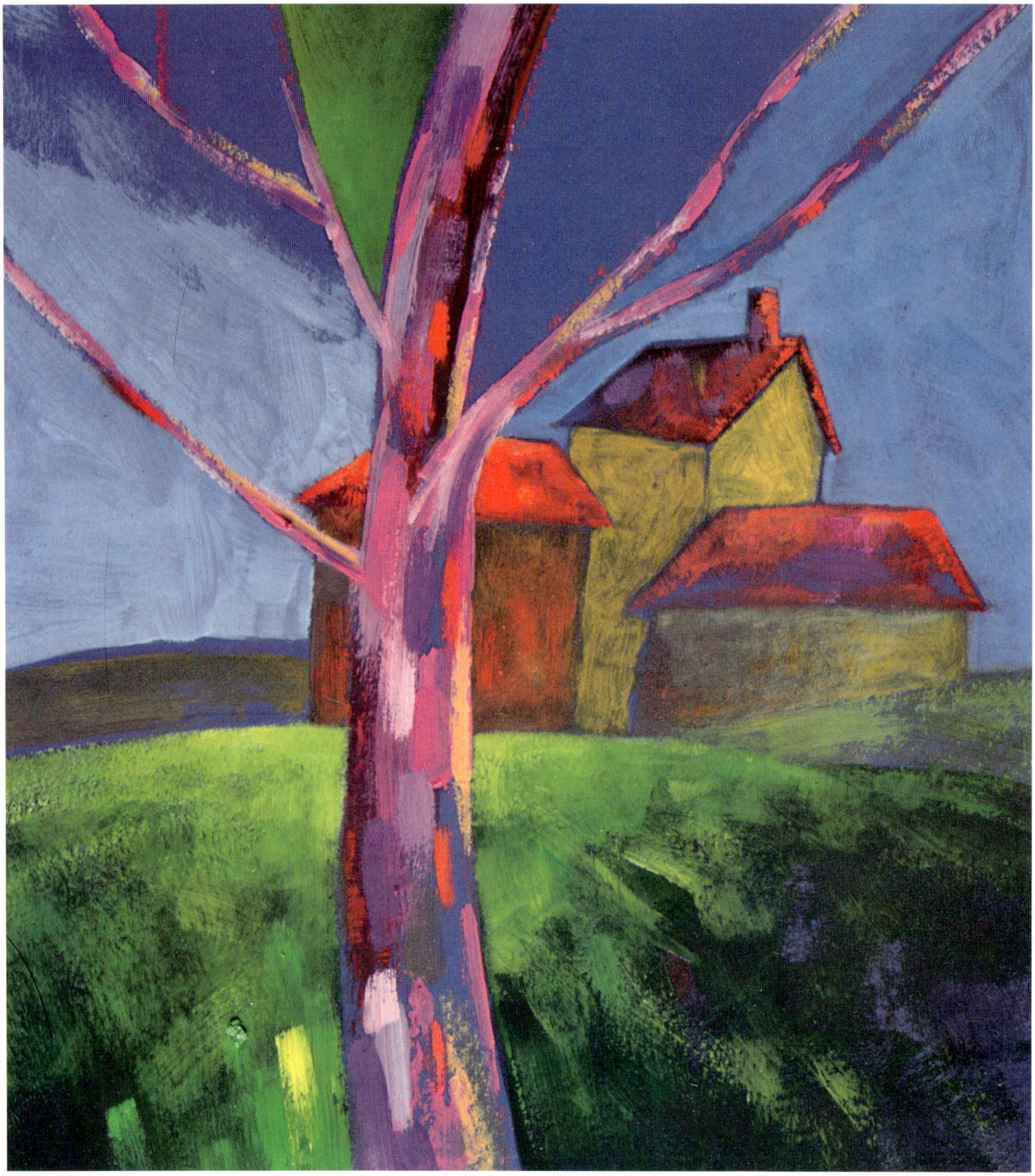

Then I intensified the tree in the foreground to create the impression of depth in the painting. In order to make the tree the focal point, I used bright, powerful colors such as fuchsia and violet, and the red of the roof is also repeated here. This repetition creates a link between the foreground and the background. Be sure you don't isolate colors. Repeat them throughout the painting to achieve a uniform, well-rounded effect. In order to create a balance of colors, it was also important to repeat the green of the meadow in different locations, so I painted one of the geometrical shapes between the branches green.

I wanted the colors in the meadow to create a feeling of depth. I used different types of green to accomplish this: The deep, dark greens in the foreground give the impression of closeness, and the lighter greens give the impression of distance. As always, I tried to keep an eye on the entire composition in order to ensure that each detail conformed to the general expression of the painting.

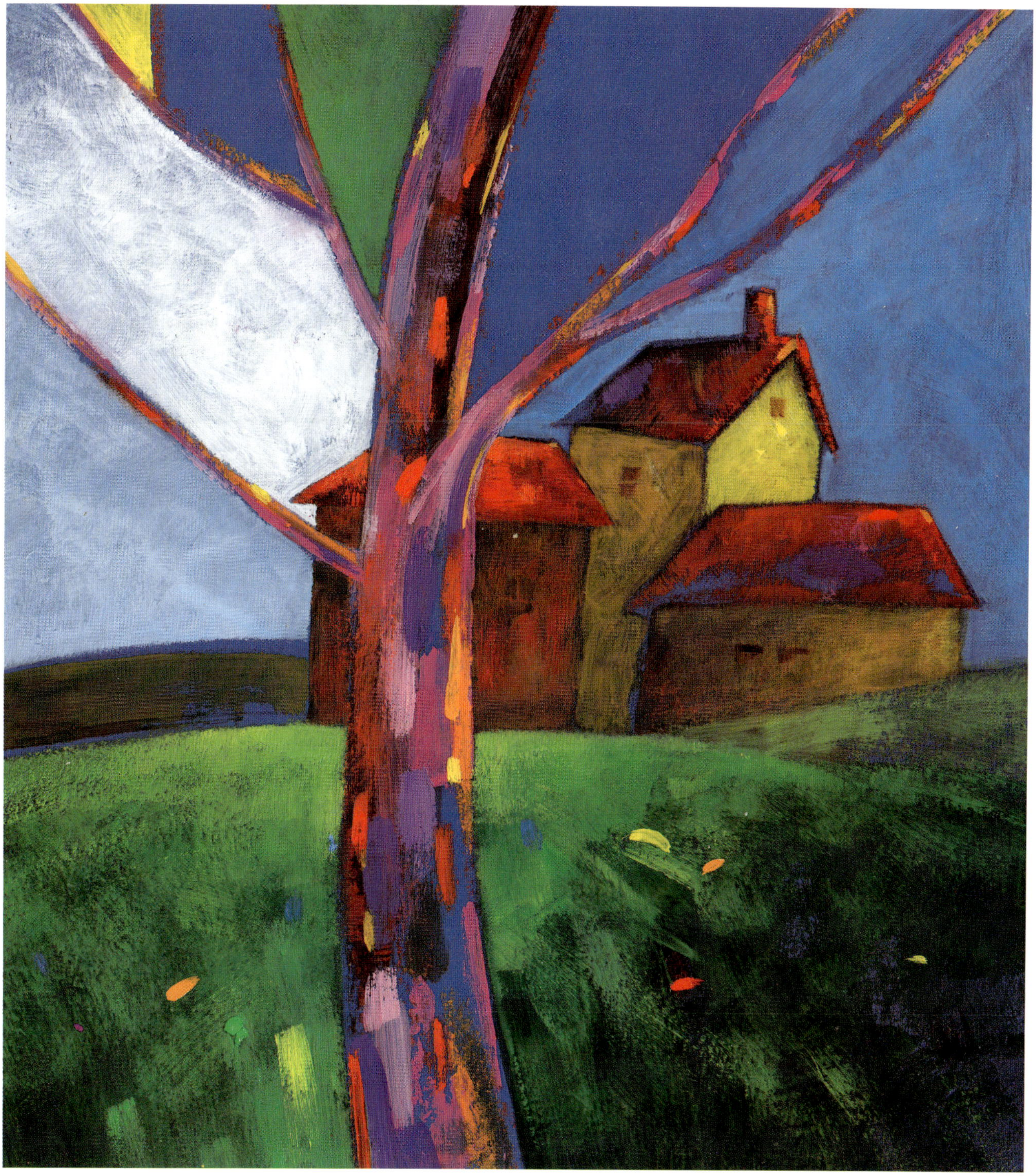

Before I finish a painting, I try to distance myself from it. I might let it sit overnight or maybe only a few hours. Then I can look at it objectively, with a fresh eye. Sometimes I lay a movable frame—two angles cut out of white paper—over it and look at different sections. All these things help me figure out what is still missing. In this case, I was able to determine that the light blue and white shapes needed to be more brilliant in order to increase the impression of depth.

I left some of the areas between the branches the same color as the base, and I added yellow, orange, and red highlights to the meadow and the tree. This effect creates an impression of warmth and happiness. I added a few accents and finished off the houses with some windows. By the way, I always try to work with a simple palette. It's amazing how many nuances and details are possible.

I was finally satisfied with my painting. The details were done, and my painting was finished.

The Path Around the Tree

by Edeltraut Klapproth

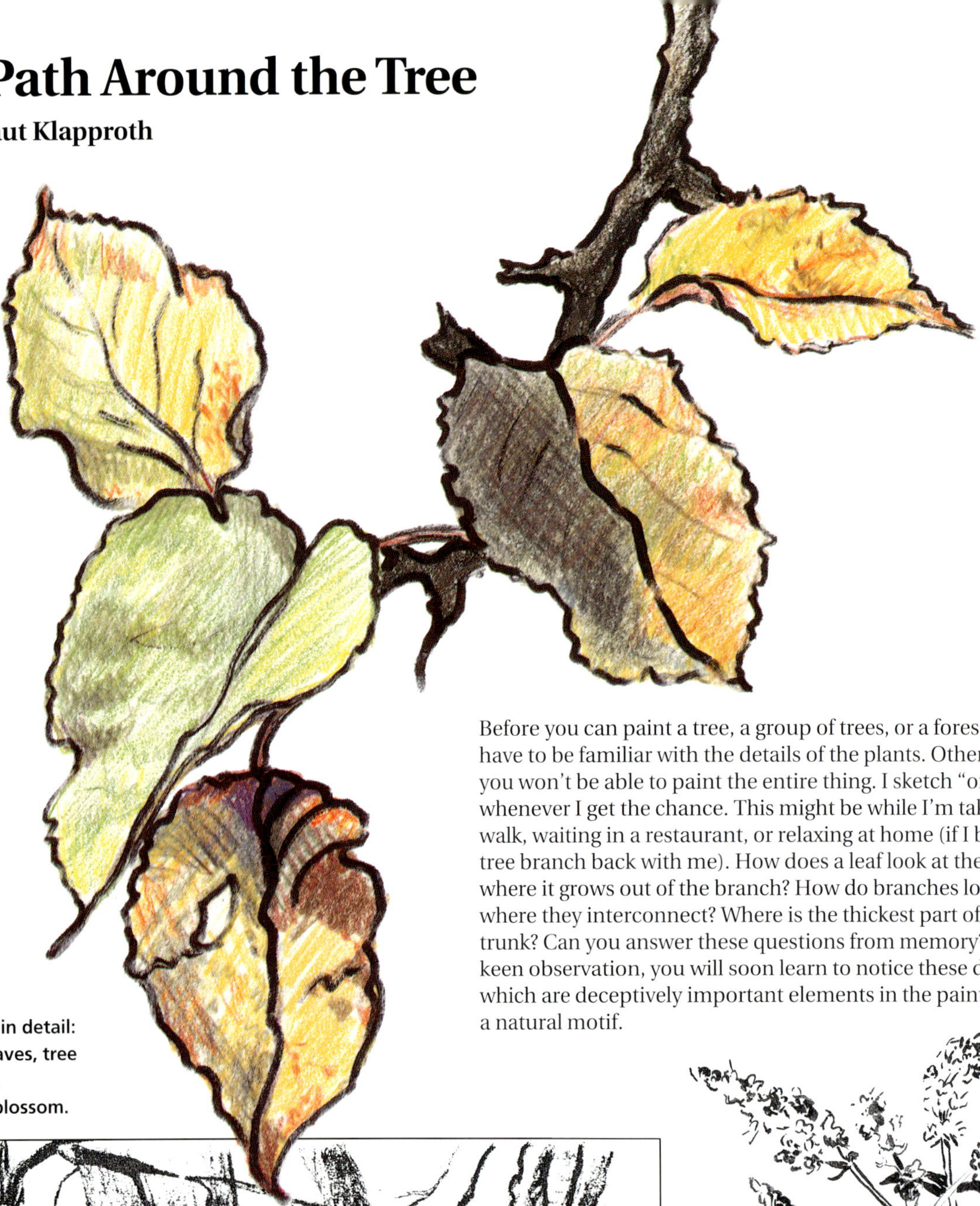

Before you can paint a tree, a group of trees, or a forest, you have to be familiar with the details of the plants. Otherwise, you won't be able to paint the entire thing. I sketch "on site" whenever I get the chance. This might be while I'm taking a walk, waiting in a restaurant, or relaxing at home (if I bring a tree branch back with me). How does a leaf look at the point where it grows out of the branch? How do branches look where they interconnect? Where is the thickest part of a tree trunk? Can you answer these questions from memory? With keen observation, you will soon learn to notice these details, which are deceptively important elements in the painting of a natural motif.

Plant studies in detail: apple tree leaves, tree trunks, and a peppermint blossom.

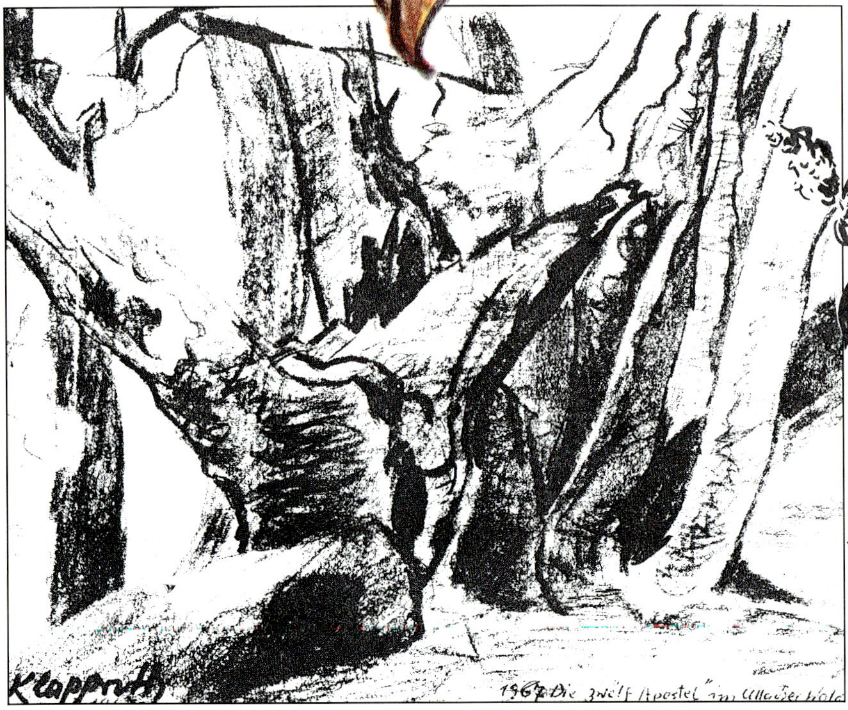

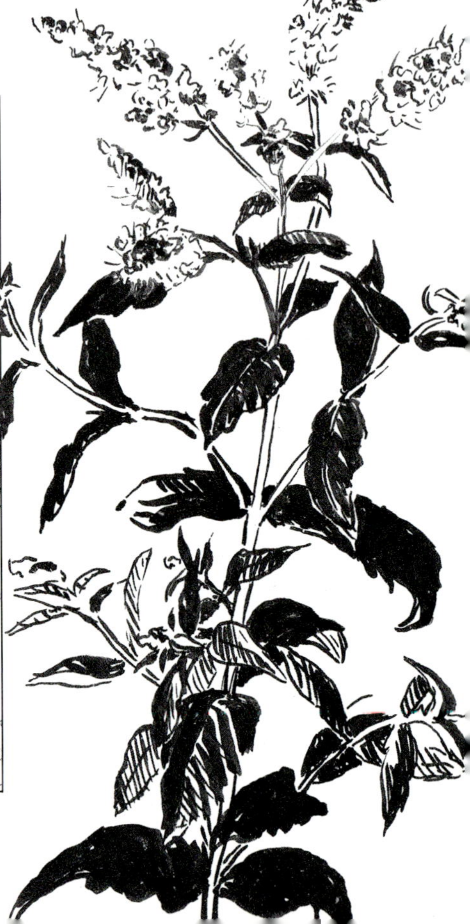

I discovered this tree one autumn as I was taking a walk, and I liked the way the path encircled it. I found it behind a small farm, where the farmer uses the path to turn his tractor around. The oblong ellipse with the dark, round tree in the middle seemed to me a wonderful motif, so I made a few quick pencil sketches of it.

When I got home, I drew an ink sketch of the motif from memory, using just a few colors (below). I tried to capture the mood radiated by this landscape. I always paint what I have actually seen, what is "stored" in me. To me, drawings are better than photographs, because they convey my own personal feelings.

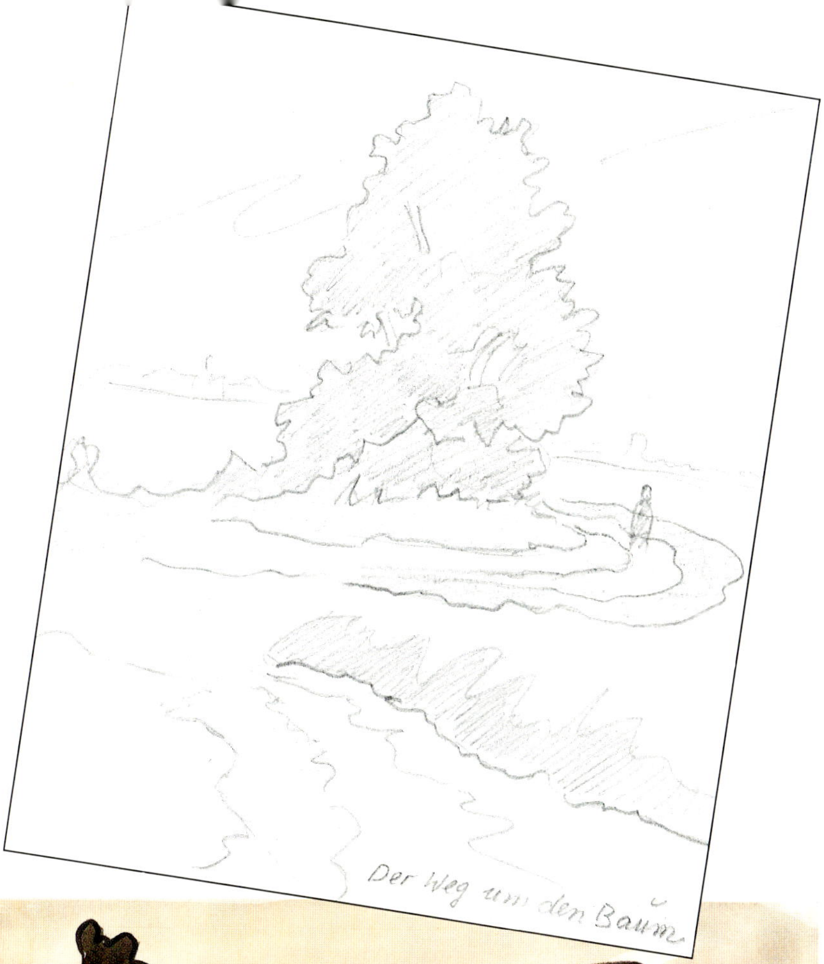

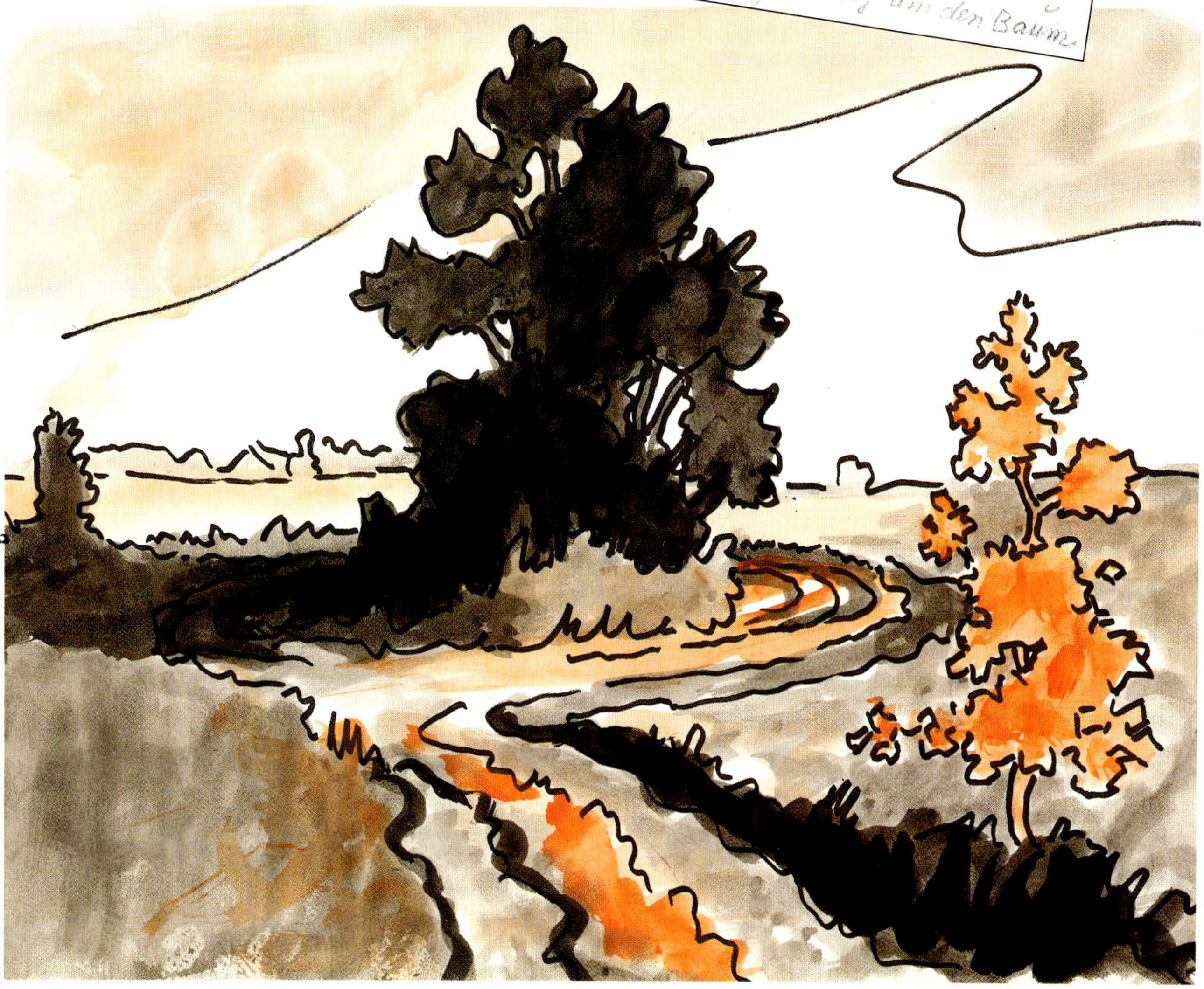

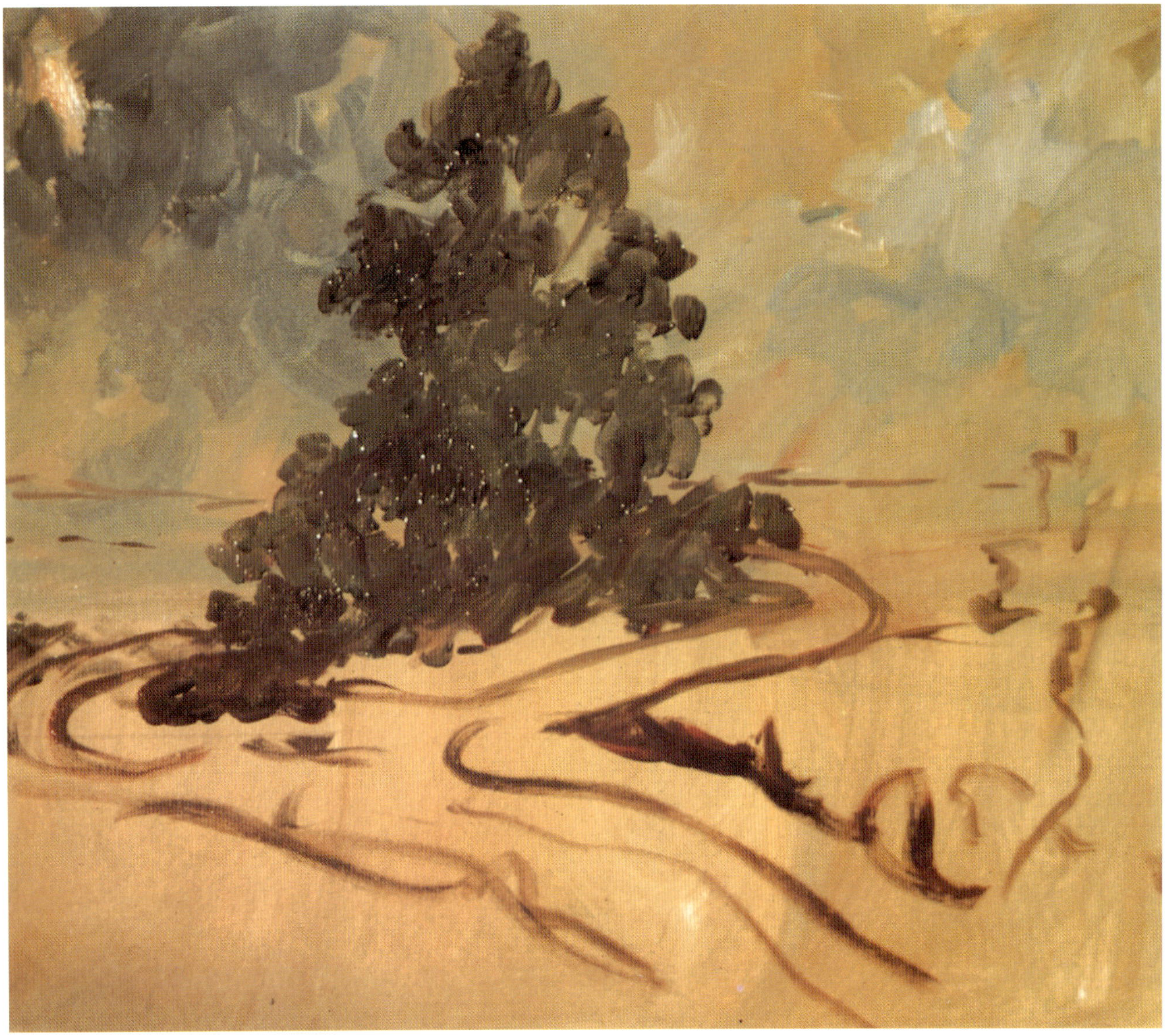

Because I don't like to work on a pure white canvas, I tinted my canvas with a light ochre before I started painting. Then I used a brush to put in the first contours of the motif. You could also do this with a pencil or a piece of charcoal, but I like to use a brush. Besides, charcoal smears very easily and sometimes mixes with the paints, which I don't care for. When I use oils, I can easily change the composition and add dark areas to indicate the overall impression I want in the finished painting.

I "roughed in" the initial dark and light areas—for instance, the sky and the tree. At this point, I still had the freedom to experiment and make changes without having to destroy anything I had already painted.

You can see that tinting the canvas was a good idea, since there is a lively interplay between the blue in the sky and the ochres that show through. I didn't work out all the elements in detail. I merely indicated the position of the small tree to the right, because I wasn't sure if I wanted it in the composition at all.

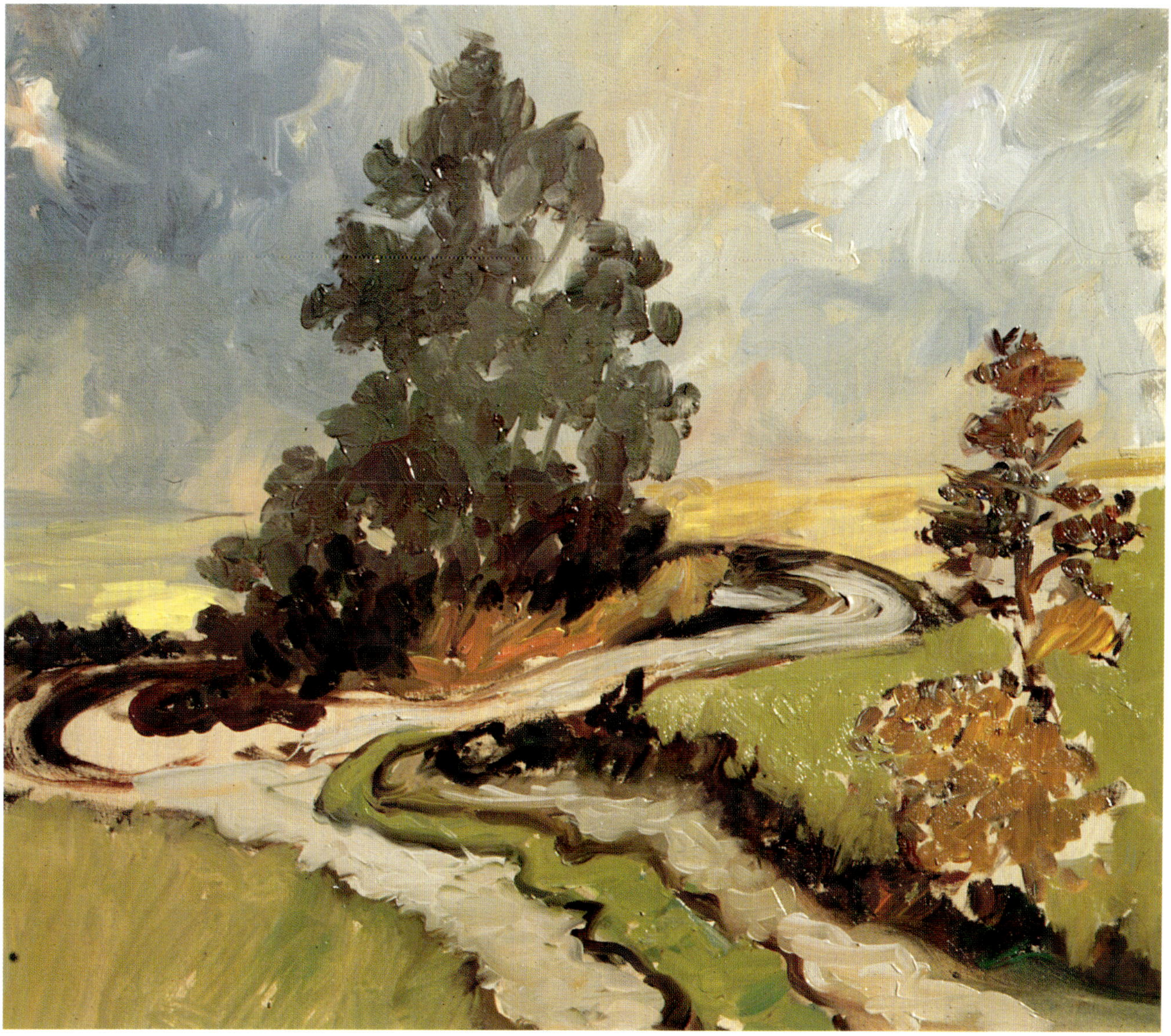

Next, I began to experiment with colors, especially the greens. What goes together well? What increases the expressiveness of adjacent colors? I had already made detailed sketches of the apple tree in the lower right corner of the painting (see page 38), but I still had to solve a minor problem: It's a green tree against a green field.

Have you ever noticed all the different greens in a landscape? Green isn't simply green. There are innumerable nuances; each shadow creates subtle changes, making it seem cool in some spots and warm in others. If you want to paint representational landscapes, I suggest you experiment with greens. Create different mixtures and make a note of how you mixed the ones you like. It is also important to notice how light and movement can affect your perception of nature. The same tree that looks fresh and yellow-green in the midday sun can seem a cool blue-green in the evening.

Next, I painted the apple tree using autumnal hues to distinguish it from the field. Here and there I darkened the colors somewhat to give the tree more plasticity or depth.

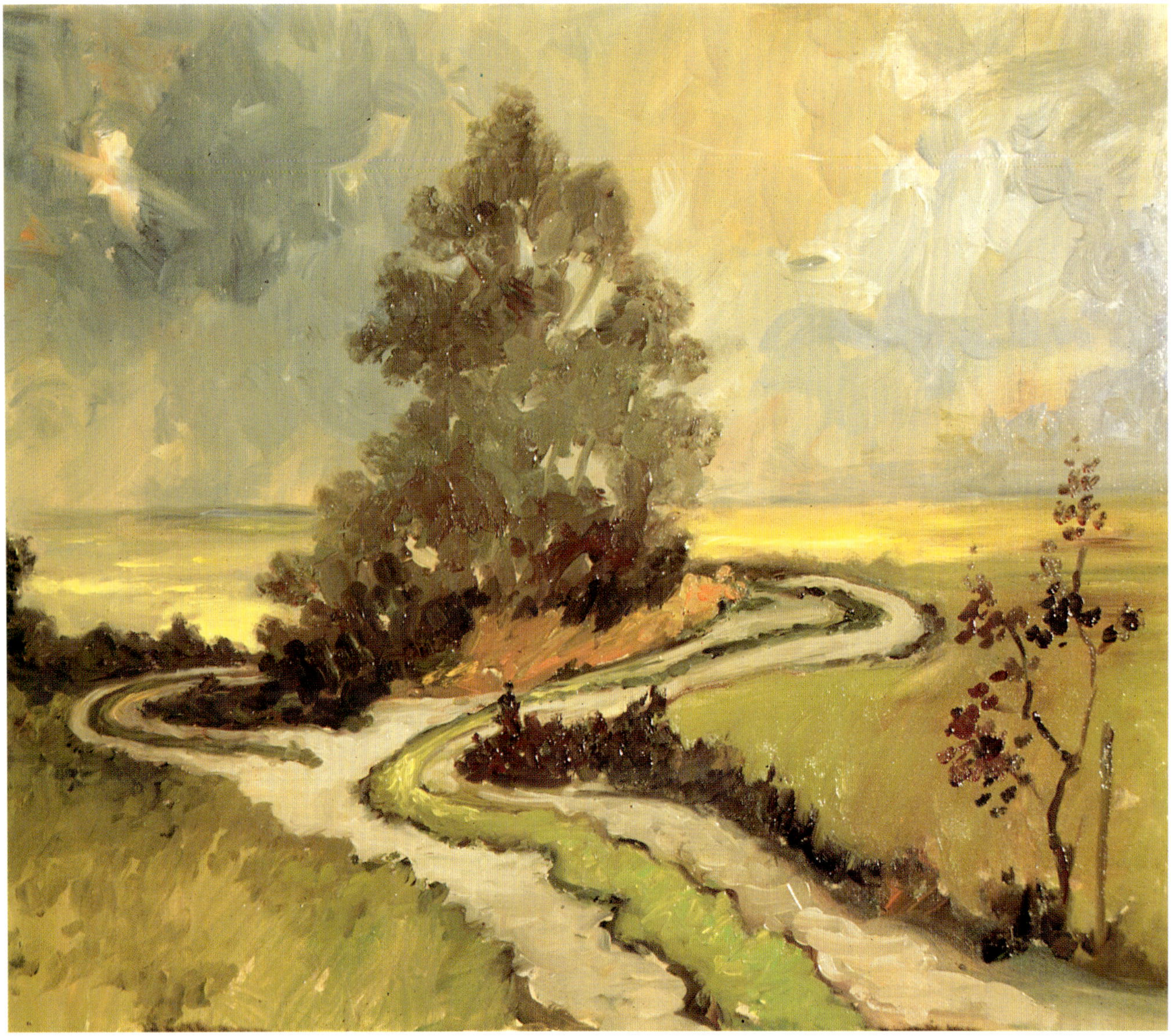

Gradually, the composition began to shape up. The important thing is to always keep an eye on the overall composition and not get lost in details. For example, I changed the apple tree because it seemed too dominant and compact in the foreground. These types of changes are very easy to make when you're working in oils.

So many colors are hidden in a landscape that it's worth it to experiment with different mixtures. I try out all the colors in different variations. The dark group of trees, for example, consists of sap green and alizarin crimson or mars violet, with a little blue-green, Van Dyke brown, and green earth. I also used these colors for the grass, but I lightened them. In addition, I also used chrome green, yellow ochre, and, very sparingly, chromium oxide green.

The sky in this picture is not simply blue. I also worked in brilliant yellows, ochres, and reds to warm it up a bit. The clouds contain some indigo and cobalt blue, putting warm and cool colors side by side, a contrast that increases the brilliant light effect in this painting.

sap green

Van Dyke brown

chromium oxide green

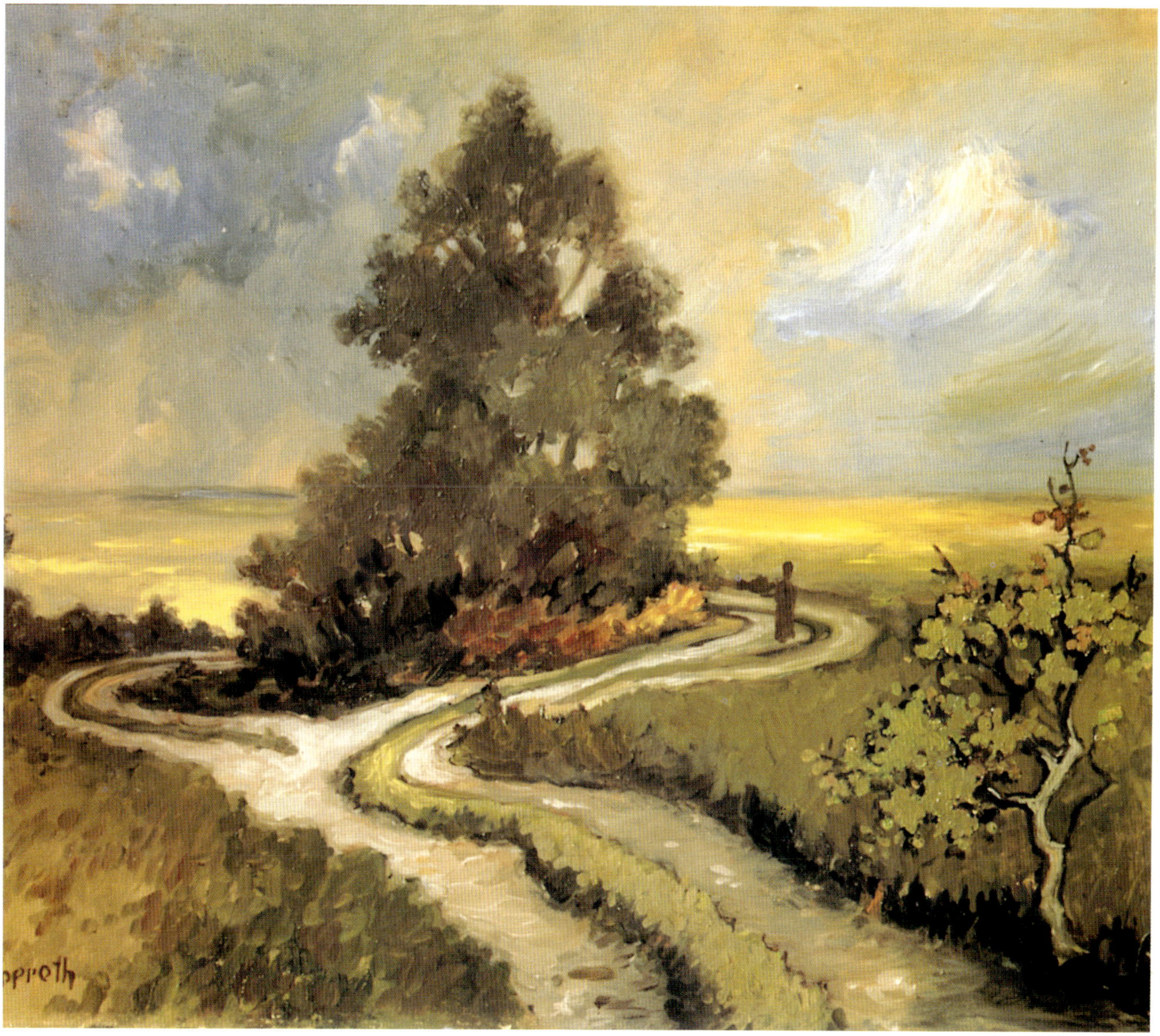

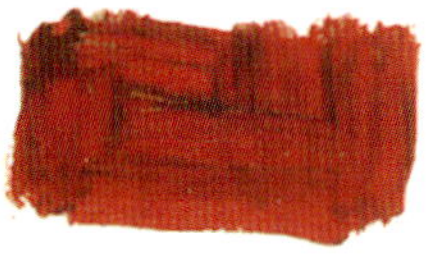

alizarin crimson

mars violet

olive green

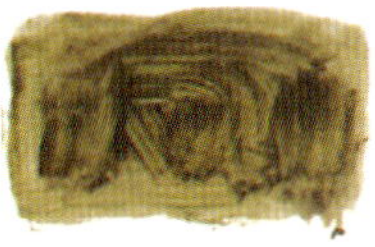

green earth

chrome green

yellow ochre

Naples yellow light

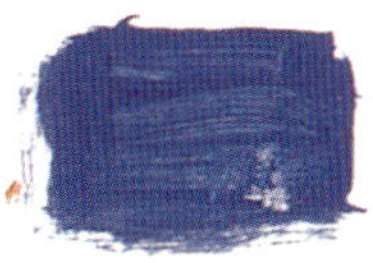

cobalt blue

indigo

Finally, I added the details. I worked out the path, refined the meadow, and intensified the tree. I added green leaves to the little apple tree and lightened its trunk.

My sketch contained a person, and I thought this would round out my painting, so I added a silhouette on the path.

Is the painting finished? I've had it in my studio for a long time, looking at it again and again, thinking whether there is anything that needs changing. At some point, I have to decide that it's finished. I like its brilliance and the way it captures the mood of early fall.

Painting a Surrealistic Motif

with Uwe Neuhaus

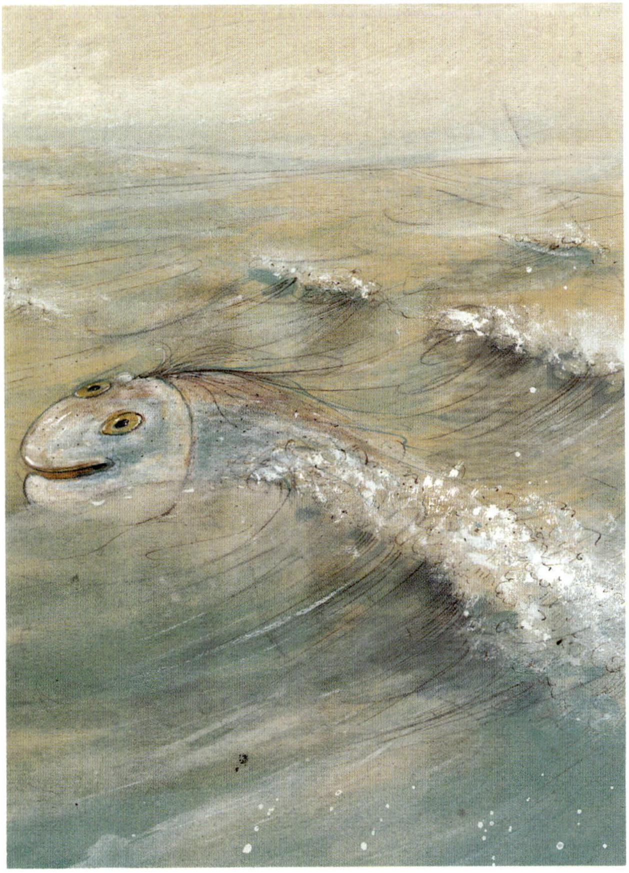

The word "surrealistic" actually means "beyond realism." When most people hear "surrealism," they think of highly detailed paintings with difficult-to-understand motifs created by painters such as Salvador Dali (1904-1988) and René Magritte (1898-1967). They think creating a surrealistic painting is a very complex undertaking that not everybody can handle. The latter statement is certainly true, since surrealism relies more on your way of thinking than on your painting technique. It requires the courage to make the impossible possible and to make it seem realistic in the process. But like a lot of fun things, surrealistic painting is easier than it might seem. Let's take the simple theme of "beach" and the typical things that go along with it. What do you think of?

Sand, water, and sky are certainly the most important components. Then there are stones, shells, driftwood, and animals such as seagulls and fish. I made a few sketches of this motif using just ink and watercolors, but the sketches seemed to go "beyond reality." After all, how do you paint a fish that is underwater? Actually, it's quite simple: I just had him poke his head out of the water. I began to think of fairy tales of talking fish, mermaids, and sea creatures.

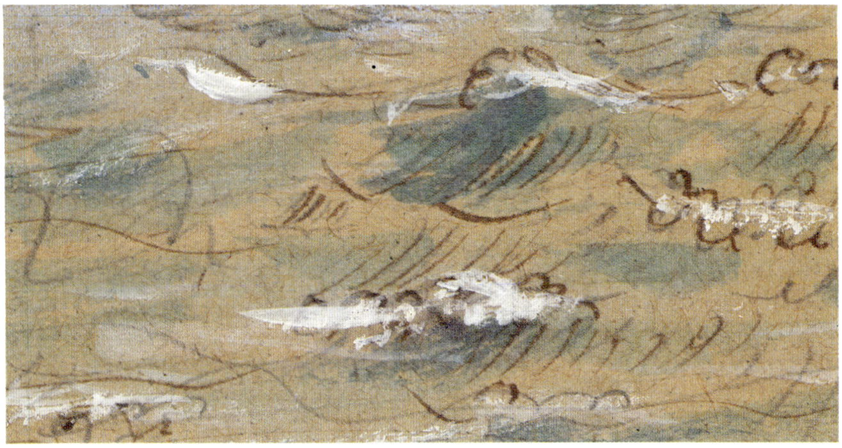

I analyzed my sketch carefully and then transferred it to oils. These simple exercises helped me concentrate on my picture and the most important element in my composition: the sea.

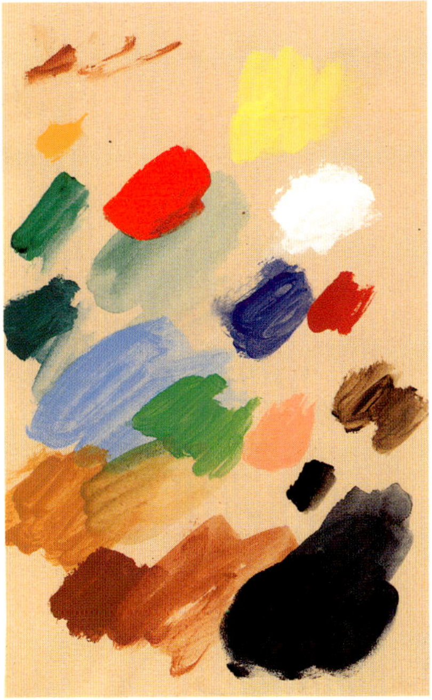

I experimented with different colors that I thought would convey the appropriate mood. Since I sketch on packing paper, I try out the colors on packing paper, too.

I did not want to go that far into fantasy, however, since I was not illustrating a fairy tale. Yet I still wanted to retain an "enchanted" quality, so I added a hint of silver to the fish, making his body dissolve into the waves. Then I worked on the water. I did not want it to be smooth and flat; I wanted waves and ripples. I had to imagine what waves and water look like—what is typical about them and how to convey their movement. I turned to my file of watercolor sketches from seashore trips for help in working out my approach.

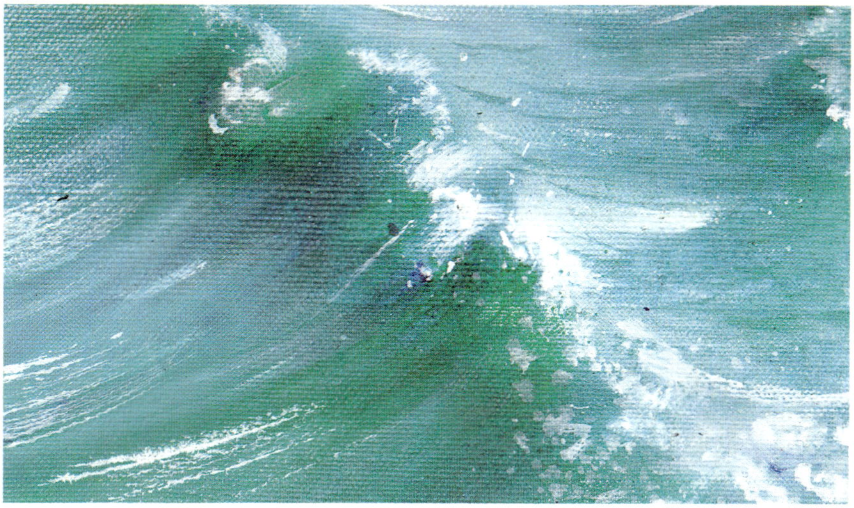

After consulting some watercolor sketches I had made during trips to the seashore, it was easy to paint water and waves in oils. The important thing is to observe the shadows and highlights as closely as possible.

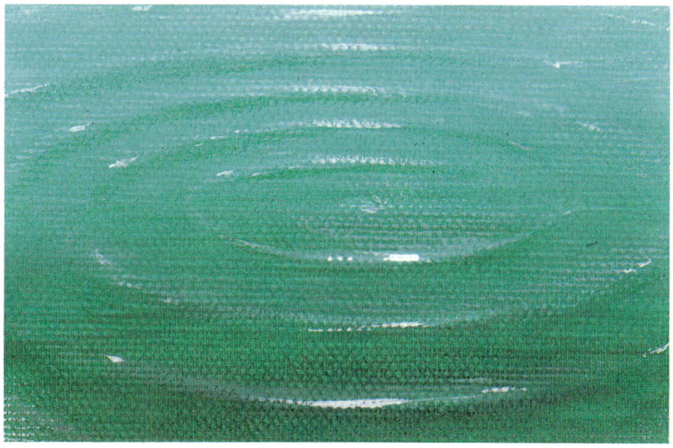

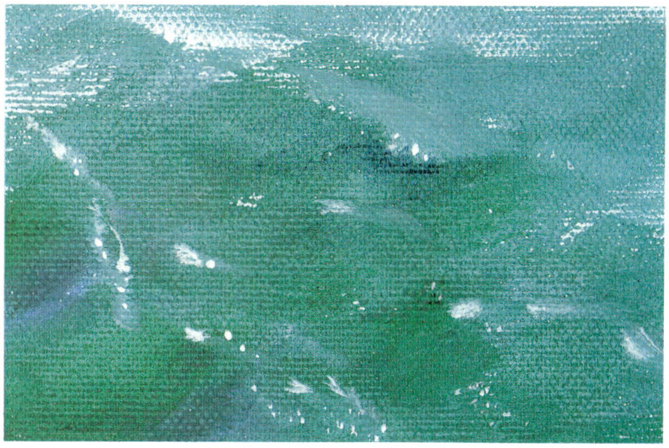

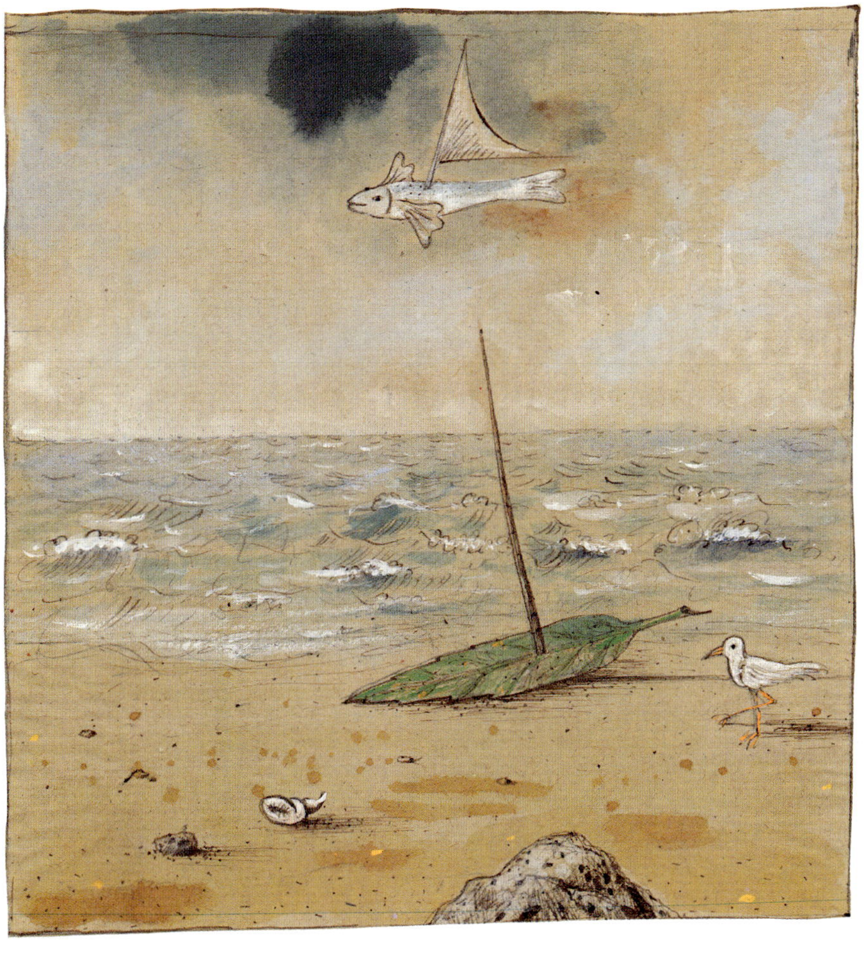

I thought of flying fish and sailboats. What would happen if a fish had a sail? Or if it were a flying fish "sailing" through the air? I liked the idea, so I sketched it in watercolors to get an impression of the color scheme. I like to work on packing paper, and I use the brown of the paper in my composition. Since I had worked out my sketch in detail, I wanted to transfer it to canvas exactly as it was. My painting was not going to be very big, so I could just transfer it using a 1:1 scale. The simplest way to do this is to trace the lines onto tracing paper and retrace them on the back of the tracing paper using a soft pencil. Then lay the back of the tracing paper on the canvas and transfer the lines onto the canvas by rubbing with a hard pencil.

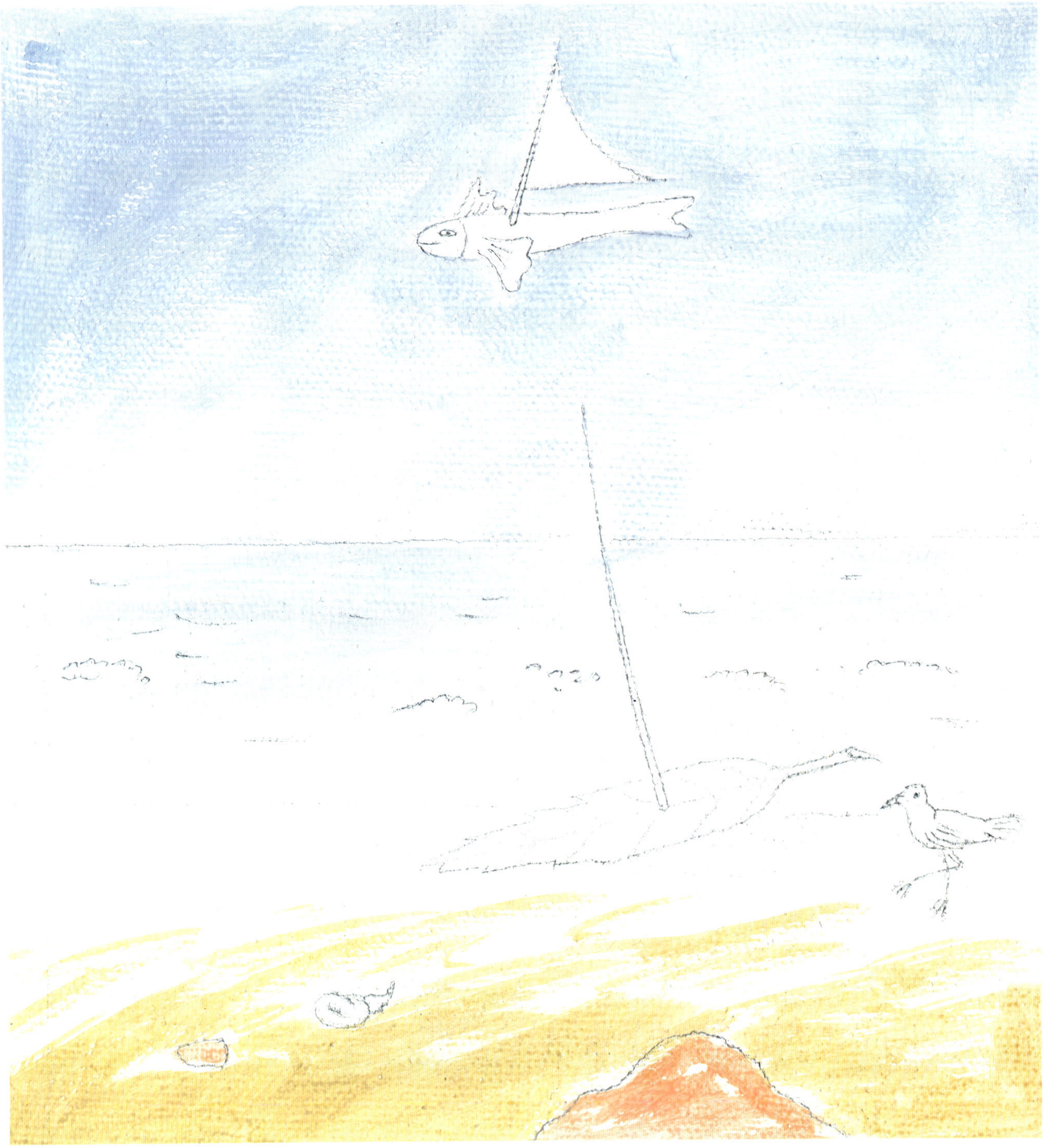

Colors used:

Indian yellow, titanium white, pthalo green, cadmium red light, turquoise, alizarin crimson, permanent green light, flesh tone, ultramarine blue, raw umber, yellow ochre, Naples yellow, black, indigo, gold ochre

I tacked my canvas to a board and used it as a painting surface. This method allows me to decide later how I want to frame the picture. If I decide not to frame it, I can just roll it up and store it out of the way—something you cannot do with a stretched canvas.

The first thing I did was prime the canvas. I used a commercial primer to cover the thick weave of the canvas. After the primer had dried, I transferred my sketch to the canvas in the manner described on page 45. Then I fixed any spots that were unclear.

Next, I put in the first delicate hues of the sky, the water, and the sand. For the sky and the water, I chose a mixture of blue and white, using more blue for the sky than for the water. I also roughed in the sand with yellow ochre. The pile of sand in the foreground was created using gold ochre.

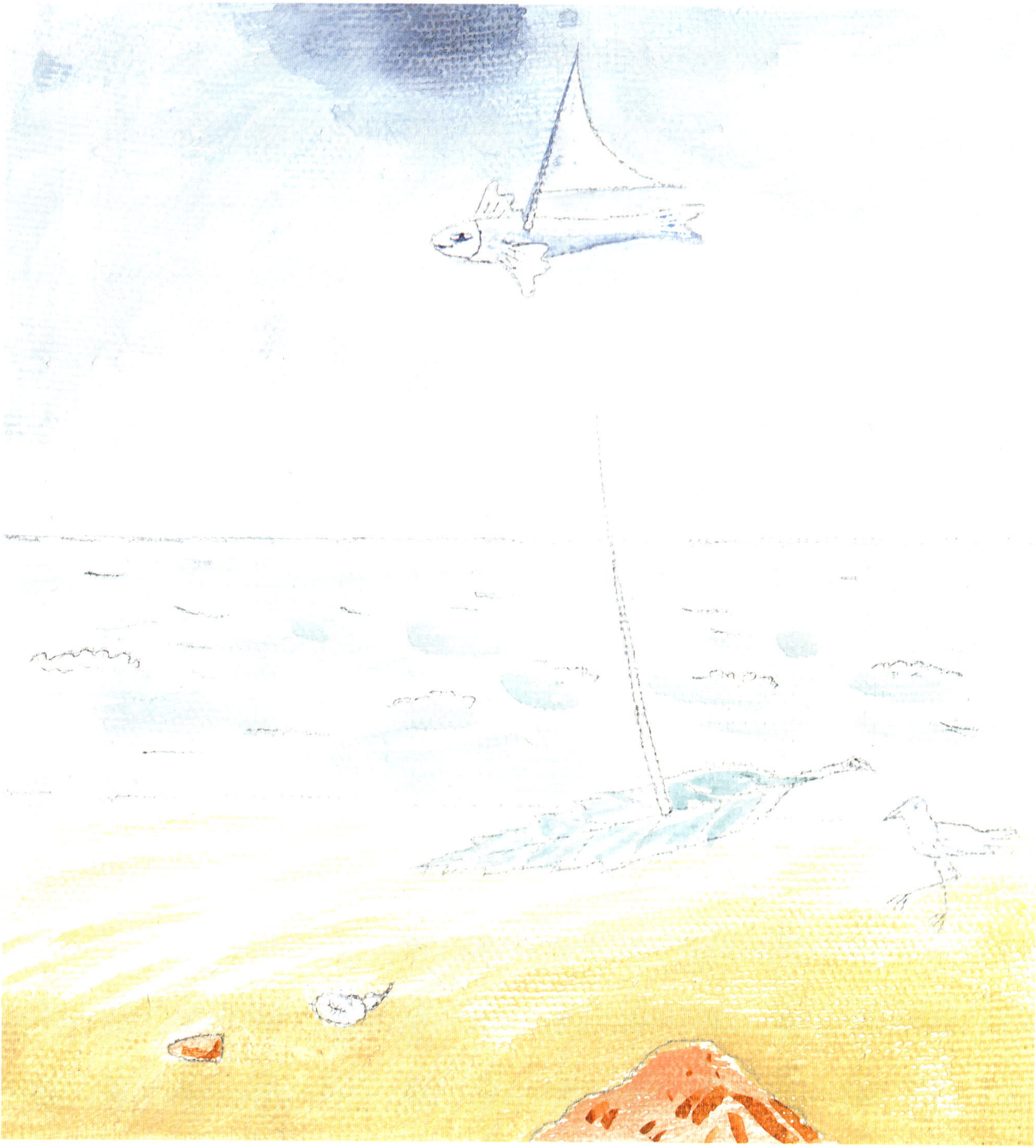

I intensified the sky and the water, adding a cloud above the flying fish and turquoise highlights throughout the water to give an impression of depth. It is important to focus on the entire picture, so I also worked on the sand at this point to provide more contrast to the water. I had trouble with the leaf, a little sailboat without a sail. Should it be a green leaf or an autumn leaf? I let the rest of the painting decide that for me and adapted the leaf to the water for the time being. If the leaf is a part of the sea, the fish would be a part of the sky.

These little surreal thoughts are fun, and I acted on this one, making the fish and the sky the same color.

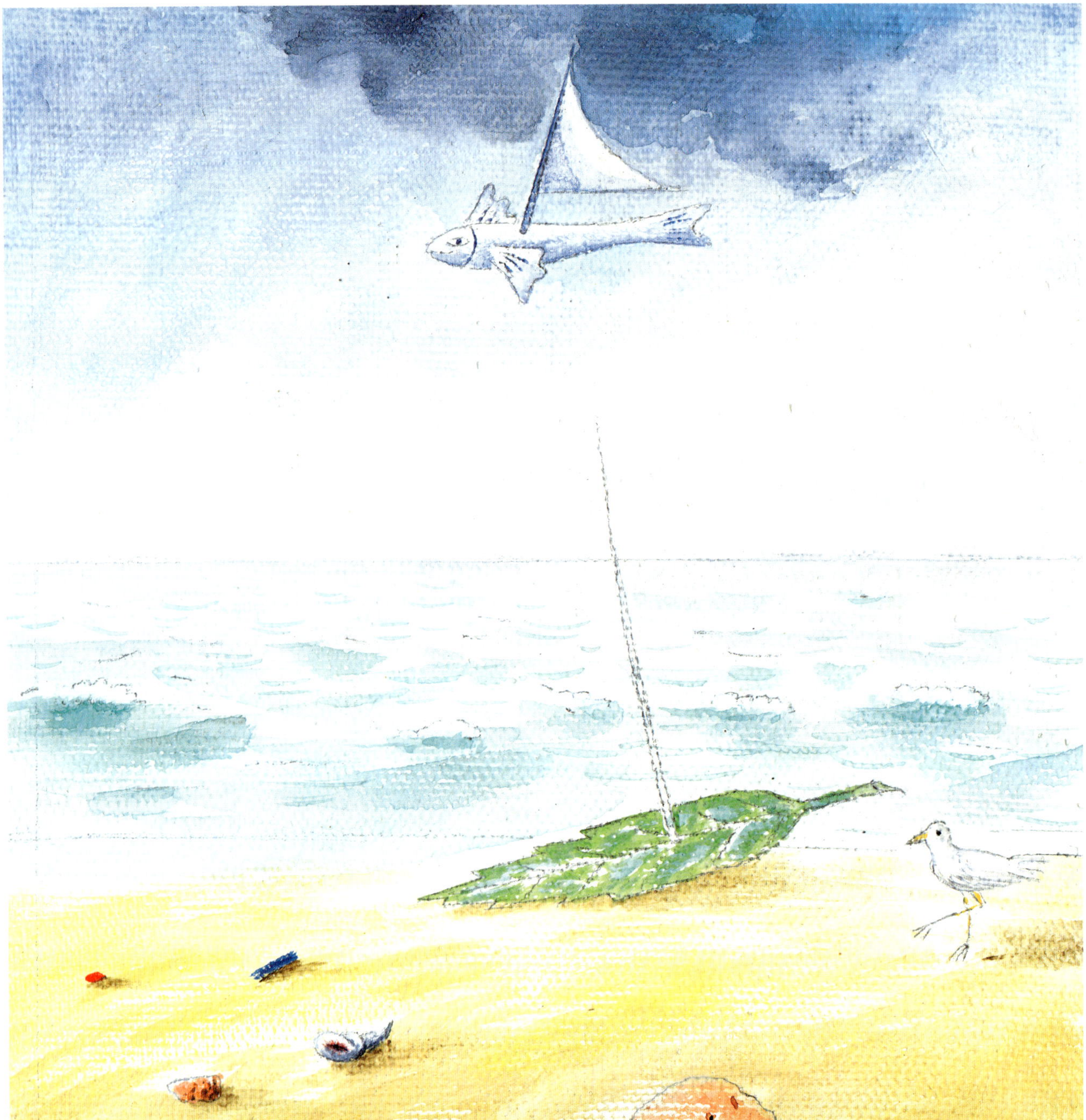

After I had worked out the rough color scheme for the individual elements, I intensified the colors and worked out the details. I accentuated the slight diagonal lines created by the masts of the leaf and the fish, worked on the shells and stones in the foreground, and decided against an autumn leaf. Instead, I painted it green, making it a summer leaf. I also wanted to use turquoise to create a visual link to the sea, so I let it shimmer through the green. I emphasized the whitecaps in the water with titanium white and used a fine brush to create texture and contours on the fish and leaf. Even the little bird gained some plasticity.

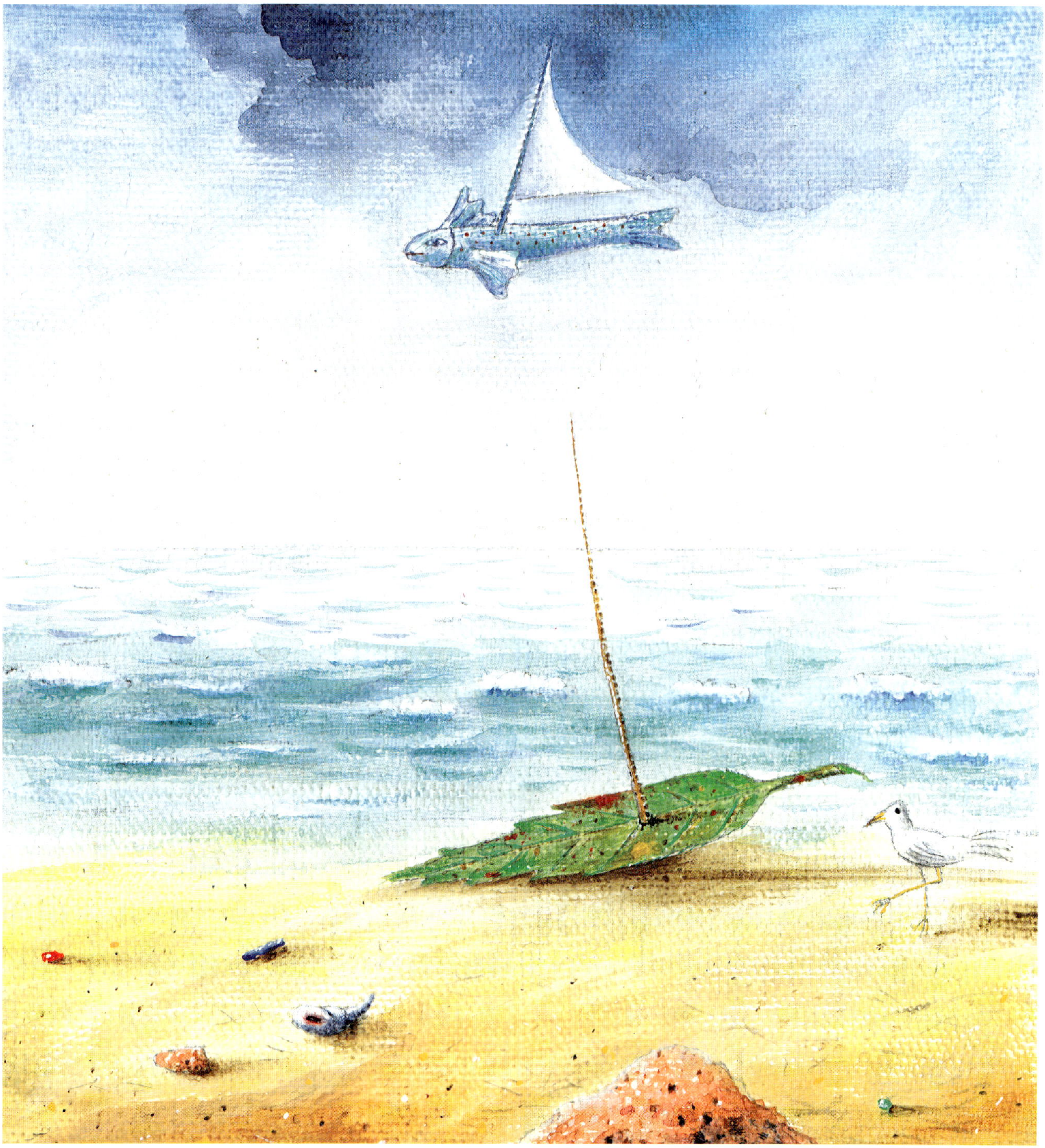

The next step involved deepening the individual shapes, adding highlights, and working out shadows and depth. The fish—the link between the sky and the water—received the colors of both elements. I did end up adding some autumnal colors to the leaf, creating a link to the sand, the earth element.

Then I looked at my water sketches and exercises once more (see page 44) in order to get an idea of the distribution of light and shadows in a moving sea. The darkest part of a wave is directly under the whitecap—that's where the water gets darker. Observe the shadows in rough waters. It is not easy to match the sky reflected in the sea with the movement of the water.

The final step involved using a fine brush to work out details, such as the dots on the fish, the grains of sand, and the bird's feathers. I think the picture tells its own special kind of fairy tale.

Painting Italian Rooftops

with Christine Meder

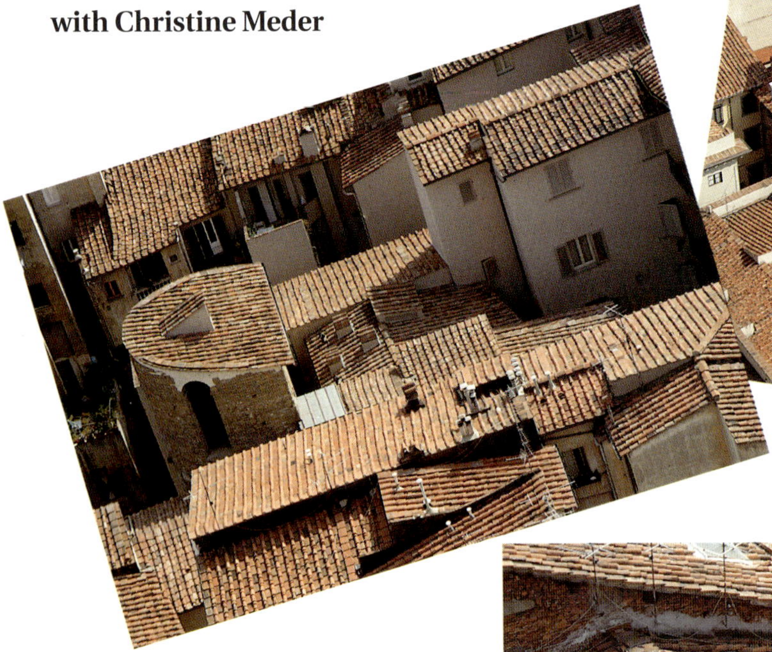

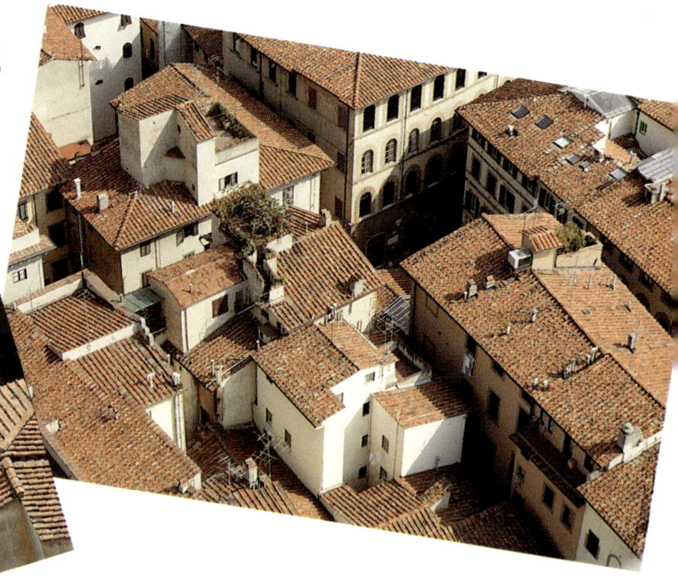

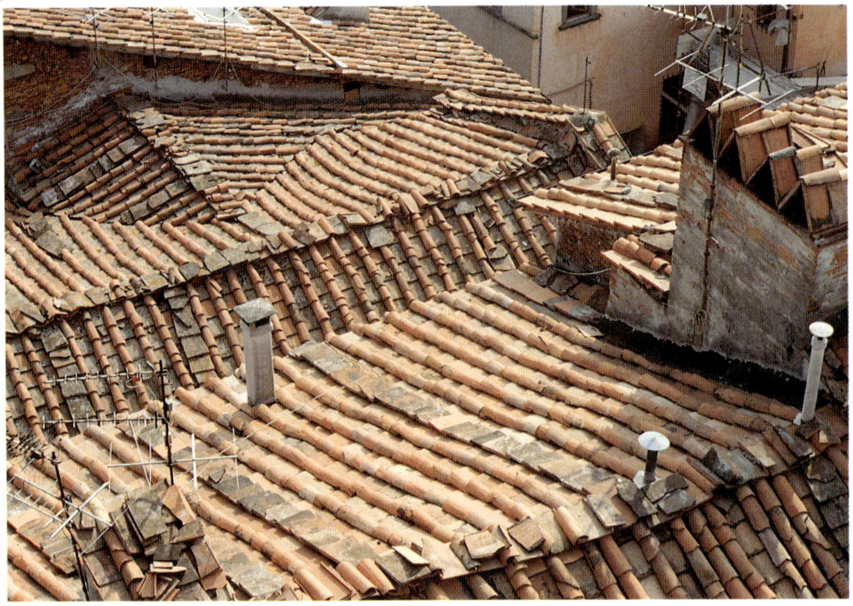

As a city girl, I am constantly fascinated by cityscapes, be it a sea of buildings in New York City or a collage of rooftops in Tuscany. So for me, painting buildings, houses, villages, and cities deserves to be called "landscape painting" just as much as painting mountains or seascapes. When I travel, I keep two types of diaries: one of sketches and one of photographs. Photos let me capture views, textures, and colors that I cannot sketch quickly but might have use for later.

During a trip to Tuscany, the little side streets and back alleys of the cities and villages made quite an impression on me. If you look at one of these cities from above, the structures of the rooftops are fascinating and hint at the winding pathways below. I took numerous pictures of them, since they looked to me like abstract compositions. Later I selected the ones that showed the most interesting interplay of space and color. I experimented with different sketches in black and white, changing proportions and playing with different compositions. Sketches also provide the best way to work out dark and light values.

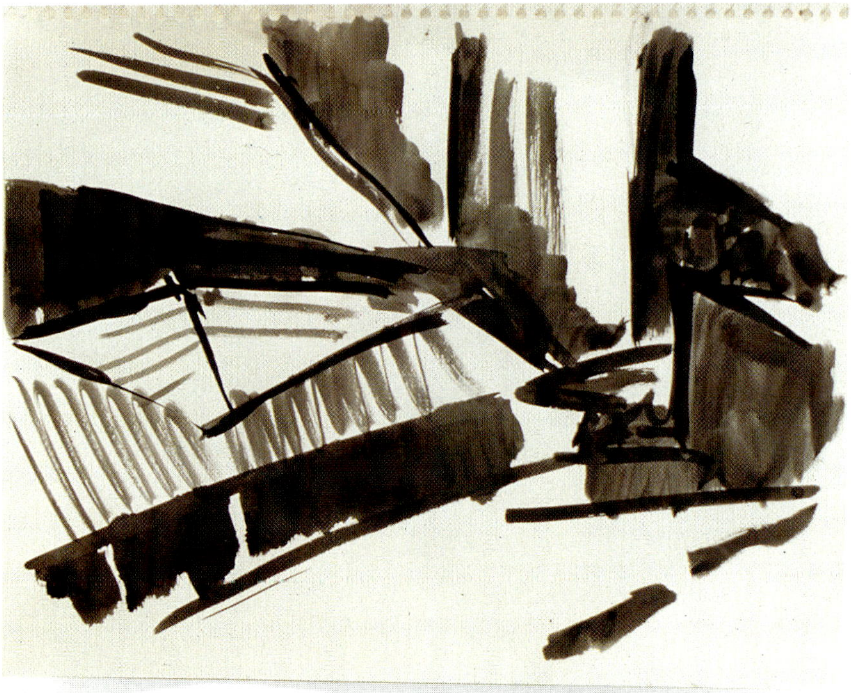

In my studio, I experimented with the motif using different techniques. I let myself be inspired by the pure colors of the natural pigments. For oil painting on canvas, I usually make my own oil temperas for the initial colors, since this gives me control over consistency and color. I use commercial paints during the more advanced stages.

When you mix your own paints, you have to make an emulsion first and then add the pigments later. To do this, you need 1 egg yolk, 1 part linseed oil, and 1-3 parts distilled water (1 egg yolk =1 part). The emulsion has to be made fresh for each session because it does not keep well. (If you want to try to save it, store it in a closed container in a cool place, preferably the refrigerator.)

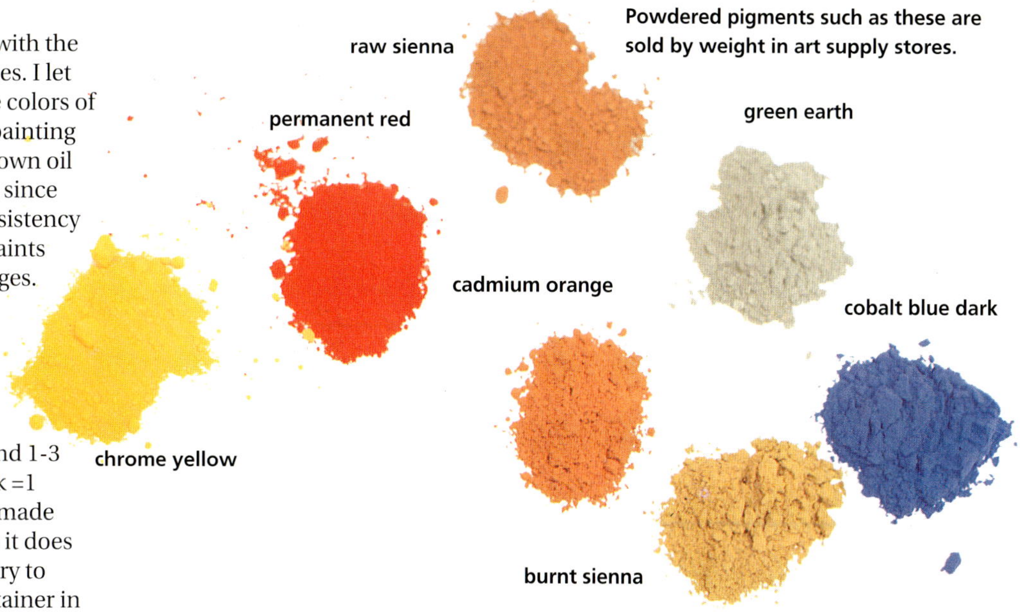

Powdered pigments such as these are sold by weight in art supply stores.

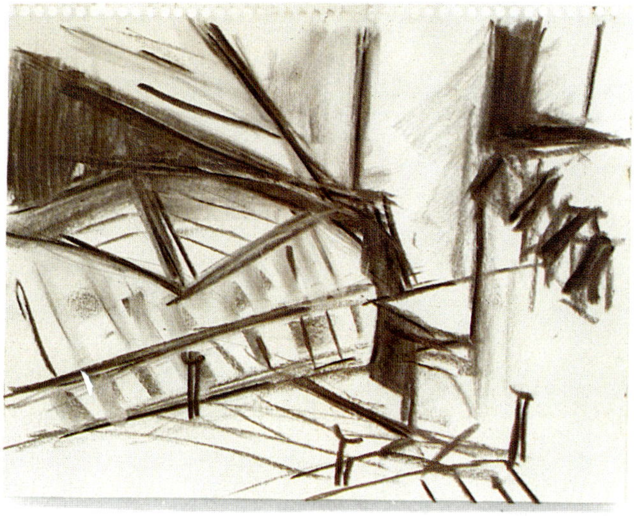

This is how I make my paints: First, put the egg yolk in a glass container (preferably one that you can seal), then add an equal amount of linseed oil and shake thoroughly. Actually, you can use virtually any type of oil, even sunflower oil. The type of oil you use will affect the drying time of the paints. Linseed oil dries relatively quickly, while poppyseed oil seems to take forever. Next, gradually stir in distilled water to obtain the desired consistency (the more water, the thinner the paint). This mixture of egg, oil, and water provides the vehicle for your paint. Finally, dab a little of this emulsion onto the palette, dip a bristle brush in dry pigment, and mix them together right on the palette. If you want to mix two colors, I recommend mixing each color with the emulsion individually and then mixing the two colors together on the palette, because dried pigments that are mixed together frequently result in muddy hues.

Based on my preliminary sketches, I "roughed in" the composition on the canvas using charcoal, which I painted over later. The way in which I transfer the sketch to the canvas depends on the size of the picture and the difficulty of the motif. Simple shapes like these can be drawn freehand, allowing you to make changes to the original.

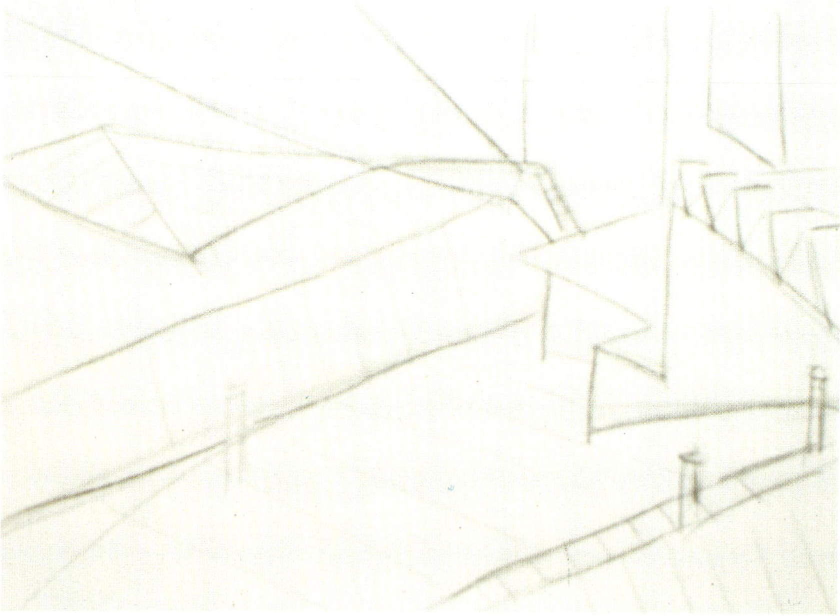

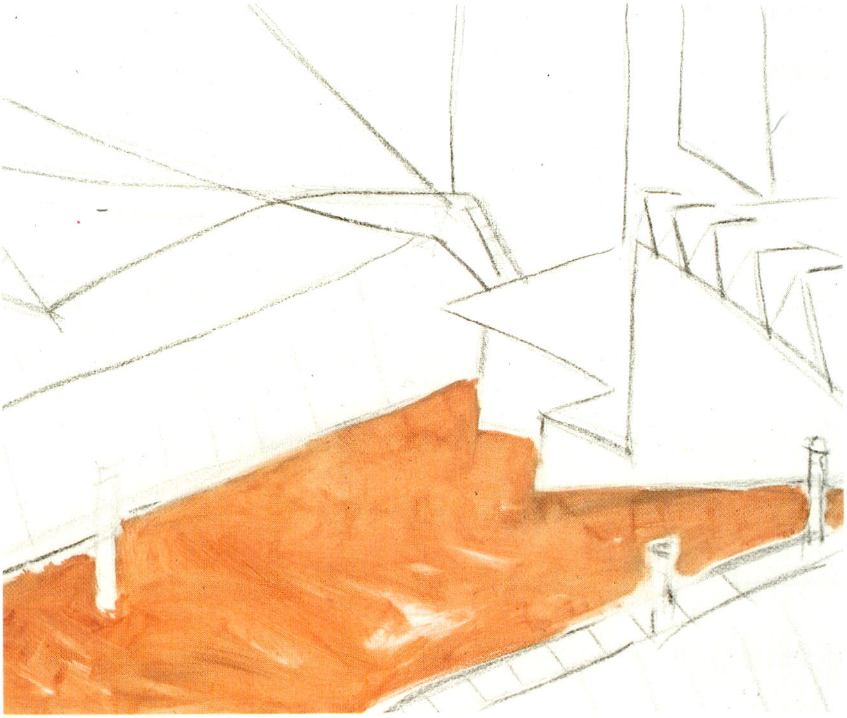

The most important thing I use the oil temperas for is to lay out the composition. As I apply the areas of color, I am already thinking about dark and light values. I started this painting with generous applications of cadmium orange. At this stage, I am not concerned at all with details; I am interested merely in laying a foundation for the painting. The exact reproduction of the rooftops is secondary. The motif seems to finish itself during the process, and I have time to experiment with colors and shapes.

The cobalt blue forms a contrast to the reds and yellows, which I definitely wanted to emphasize in my painting.

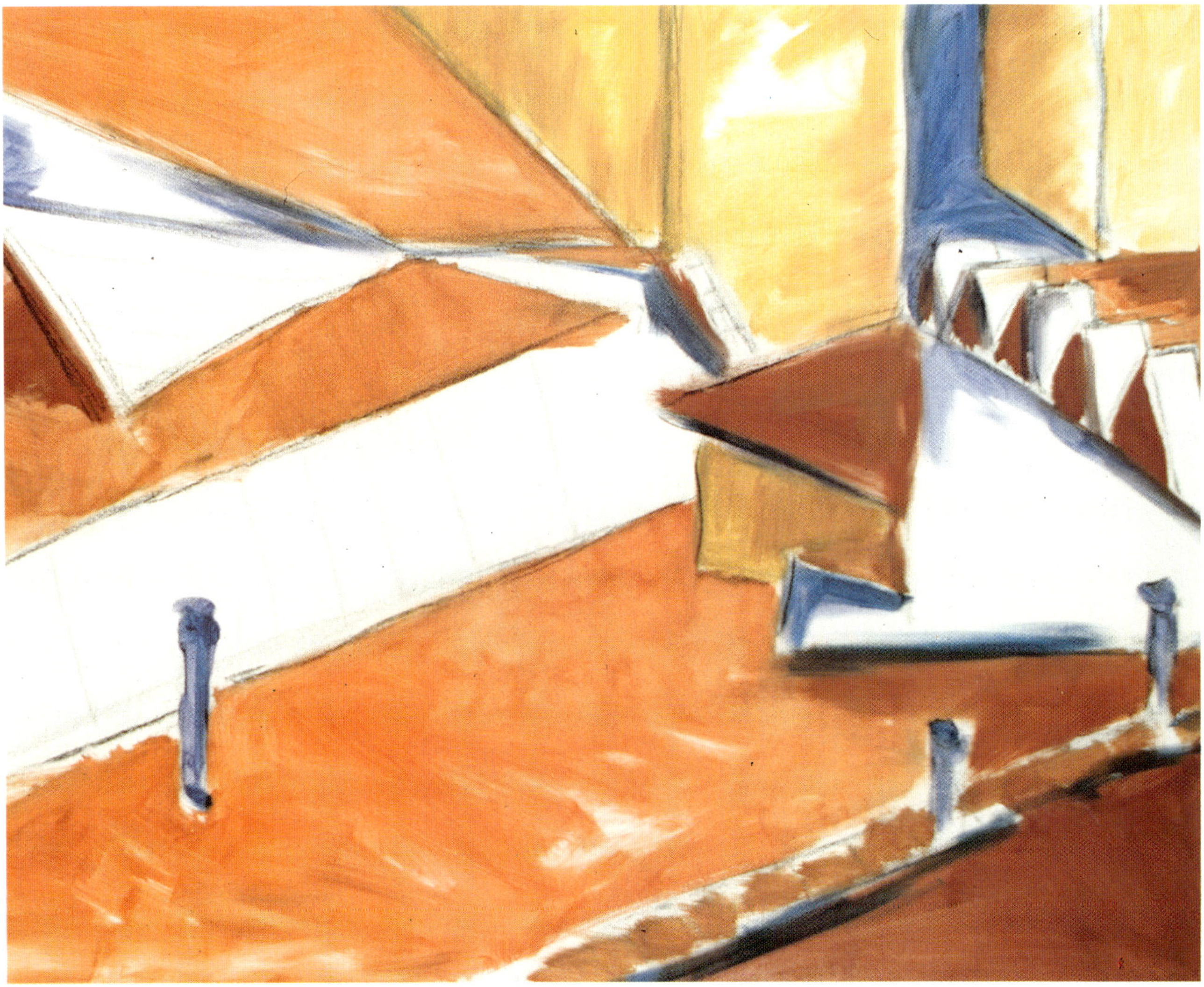

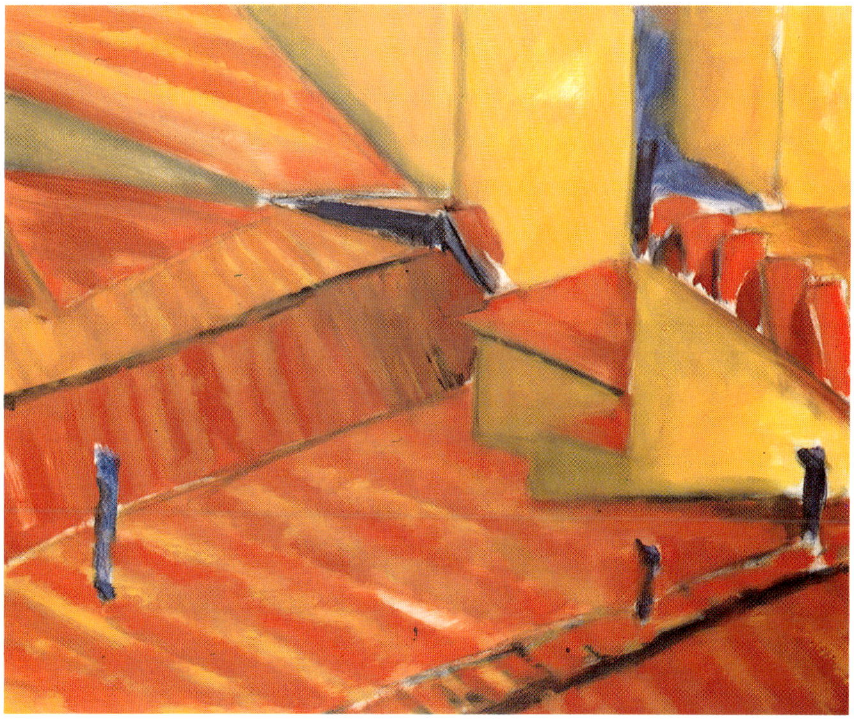

Warm reds, yellows, and browns are typical of many Italian cities. The yellow rounds out the reds, accentuating the impression of warmth due to the contrast with the cool blue. Next, I worked on the textures in the rooftops. The important thing to me was the pattern of the lines that run in all different directions, not the individual tiles. In order to apply the dark and light values, I referred to the original photograph, constantly comparing and making corrections.

After I had determined the basic color scheme, I began to work with oil paints from the tube. I painted individual walls with titanium white, allowing the background to lightly shimmer through. The individual areas were planned out—not just painted randomly—which adds liveliness and movement to the colors.

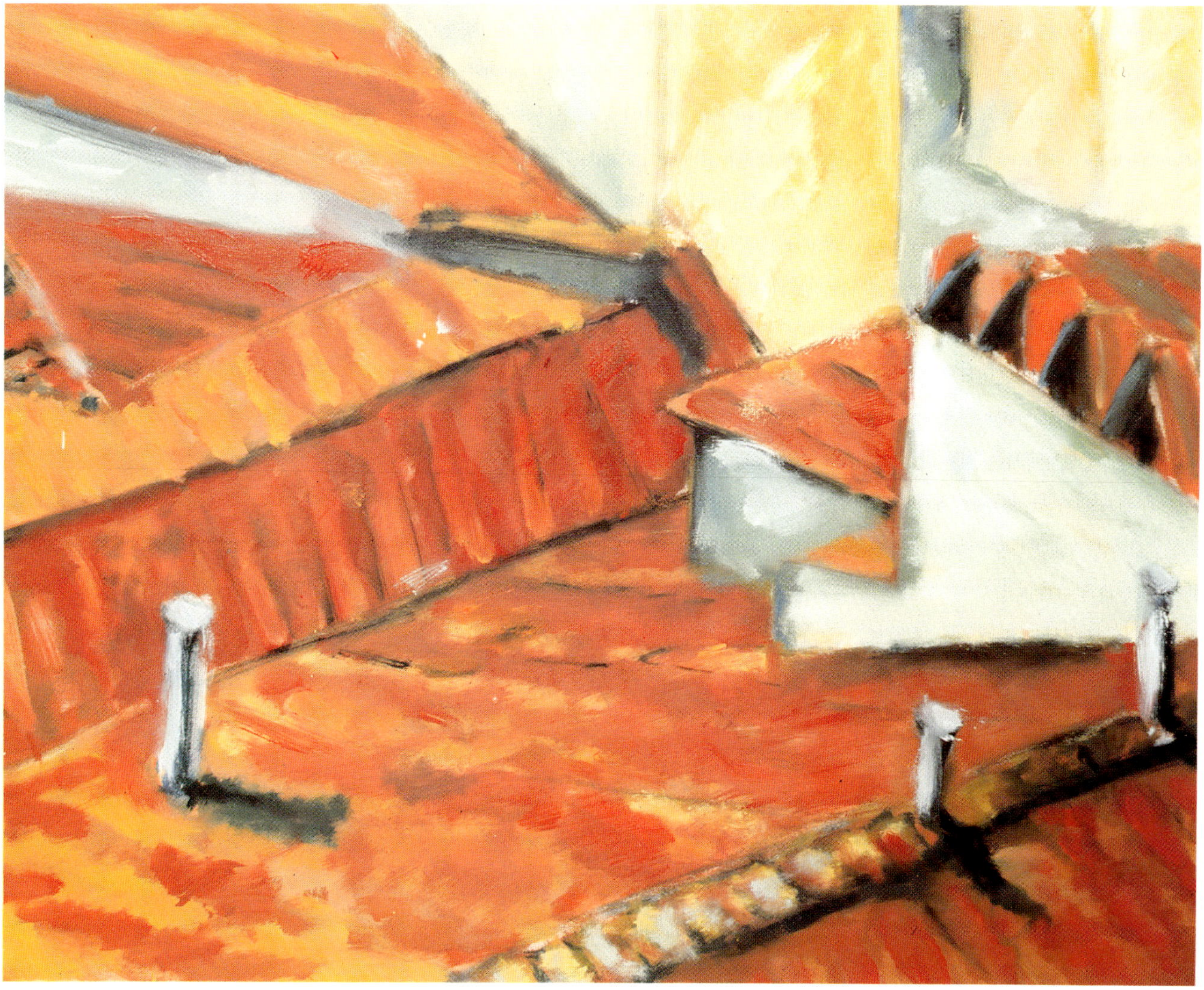

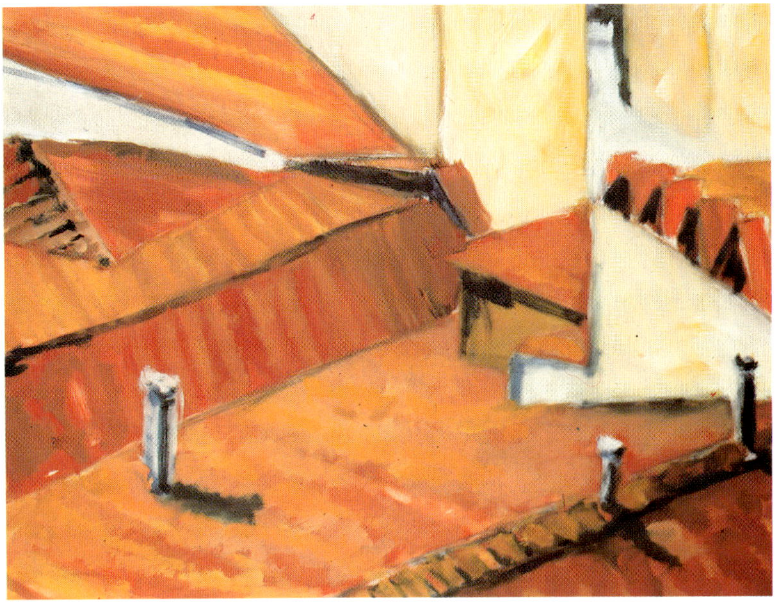

Except for the preliminary work, I do not follow a predetermined sequence of events when I paint. I experiment, make sketches, and start over. This continuous change is my favorite aspect of oil painting.

Step back from your painting every now and then to gain some distance from it. You can often see something the next day that you overlooked the evening before. The oil temperas, by the way, can blend with the oil paints, even after they have dried, which can create very nice effects.

Compare the different stages of the motif, the way I worked out light and shadows. What would you have done differently?

In the painting above, I suddenly felt the white wall was too warm. I wanted more contrast, so I went over it with cobalt blue (right).

Sometimes I put a piece of colored paper on the canvas (it sticks in the wet paint) to try out different hues. This will spare you the trouble of painting over a color if you do not like it. By the way, using a piece of colored paper was not my invention—the old masters and well-known artists such as Picasso were doing it long ago.

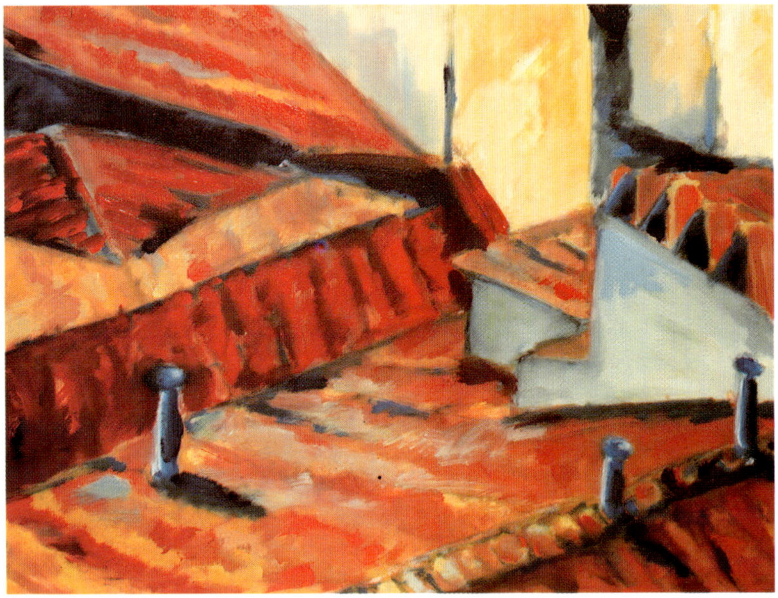

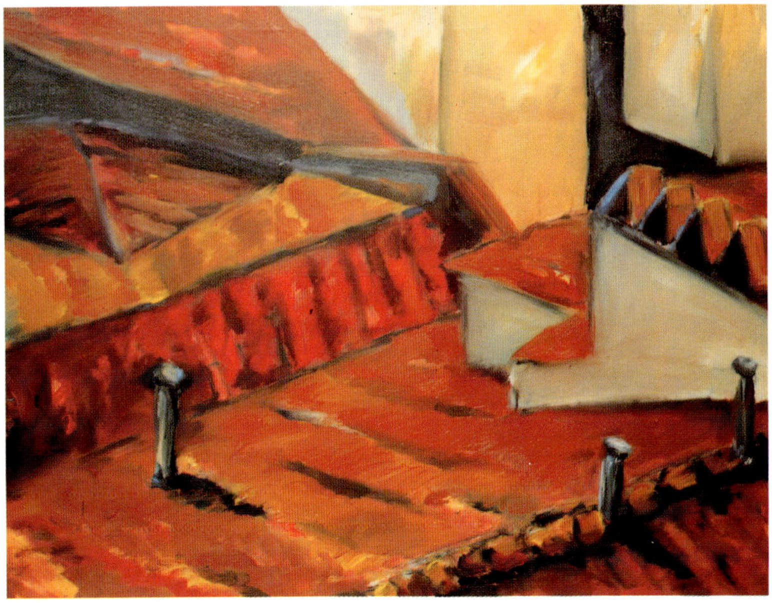

After I had worked out the textures of the rooftops, and the areas had become less turbulent, the cool, dark wall seemed too isolated, as if it were falling out of the composition (above). By going over it with a warm yellow, I was able to incorporate it back into the painting. It's also important to me that the background color shimmer through, so the various sections don't appear "dead."

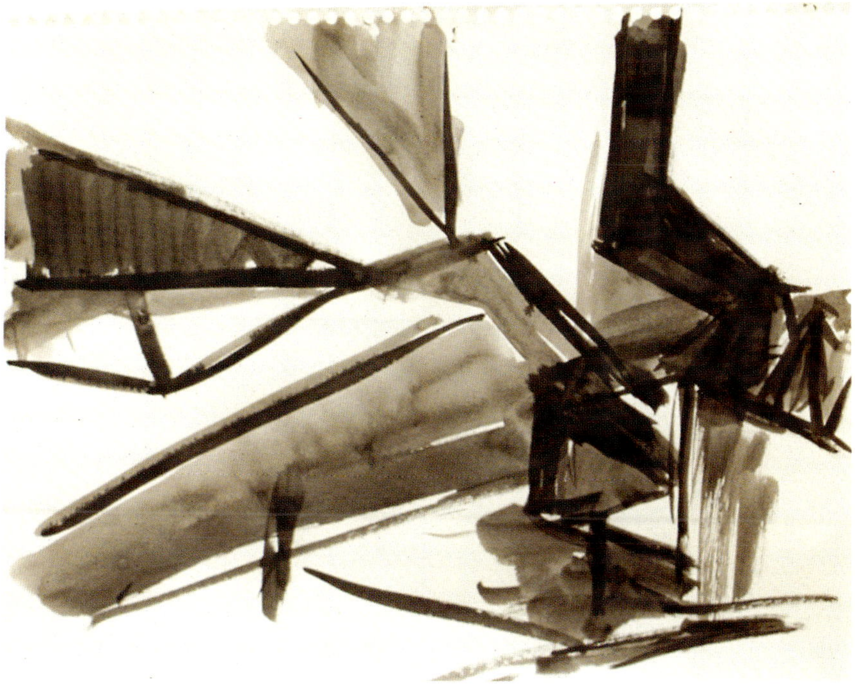

I make sketches while I am working as well as before I start a painting. I try out different compositions. The sketches are frequently abstract and form individual compositions of their own. I work with an idea of what I want to express, but I do not have any hard and fast ideas of how the final painting should look.

The final step always involves making refinements. I finished off the textures, changed the light on the chimney, added a few highlights, and then left the painting alone for a while.

For now, I do not want to change anything about the painting. It expresses everything I wanted it to. But this does not mean I won't change my mind in two or three days.

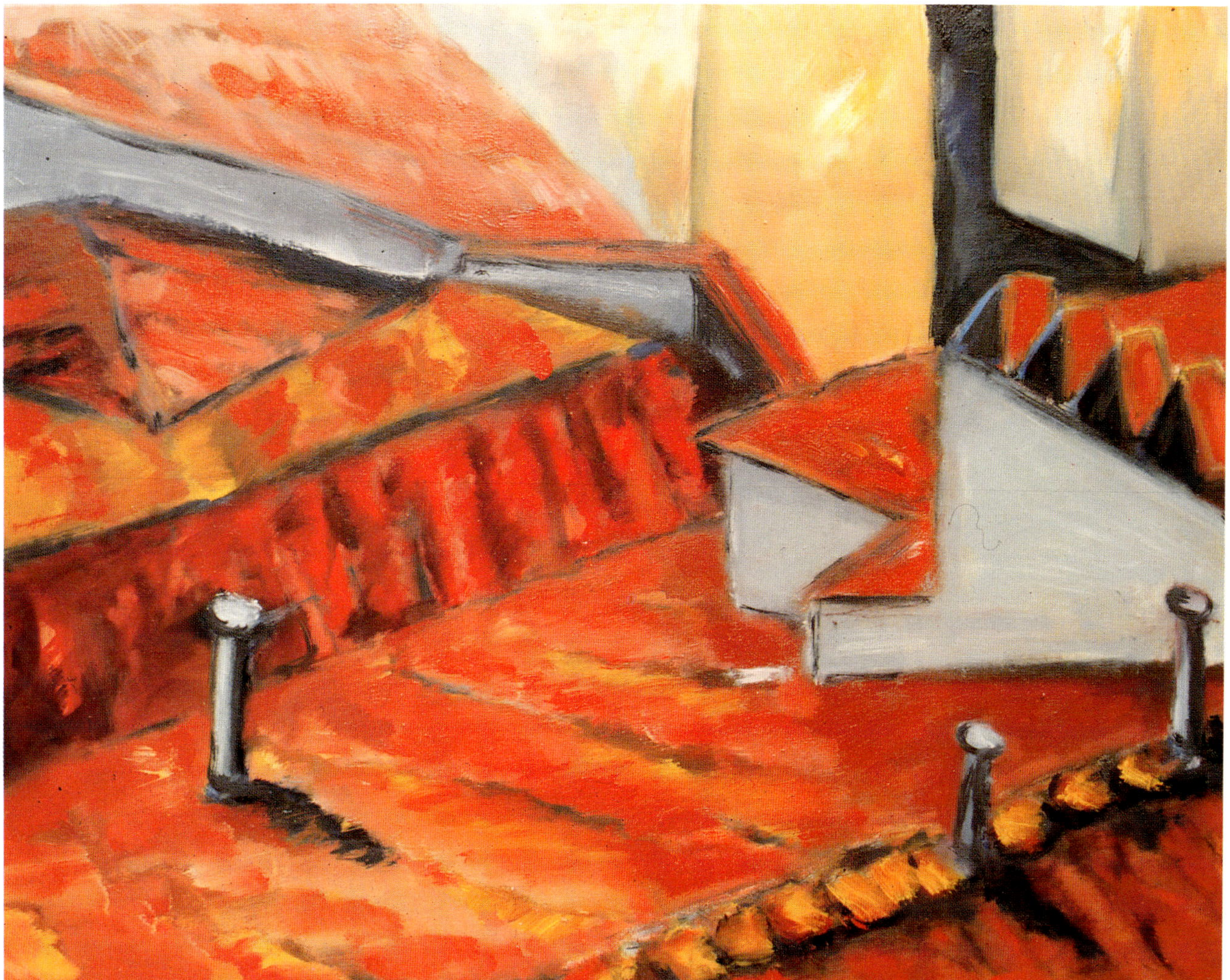

Experiments

Painting should be fun—and that means allowing yourself to try something a bit unusual if you want. Try experimenting with the leftover paint you often have on your palette at the end of a project. If something turns out particularly well, make a note of how you did it so you can do it again later. In the example to the right, too much green was left on the palette, so the artist thinned it and applied it like a base coat to use for experiments. You can draw in it, paint over it, press corrugated cardboard onto it—you get a different texture each time. In this example, the artist took some corrugated cardboard, painted the ridges yellow and pressed it onto the painted background. This is a good way to depict picket fences or fabric patterns.

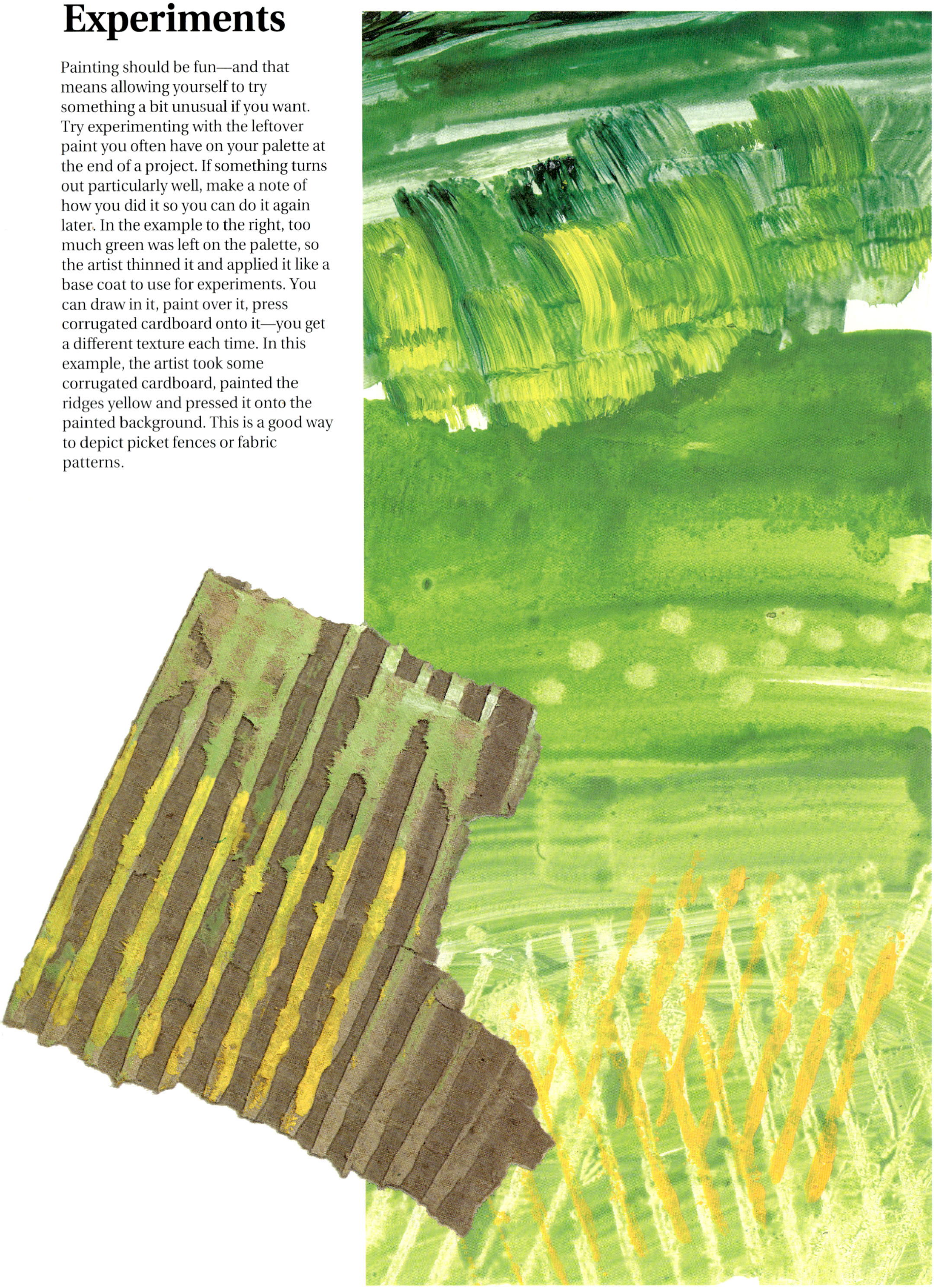

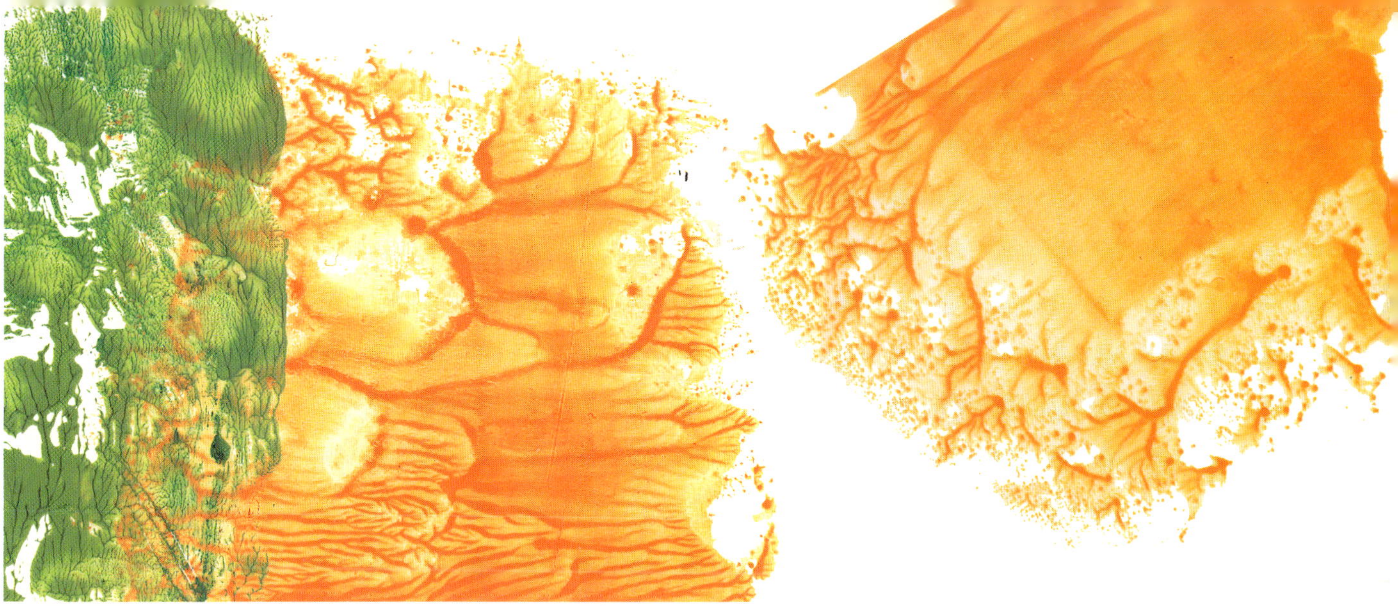

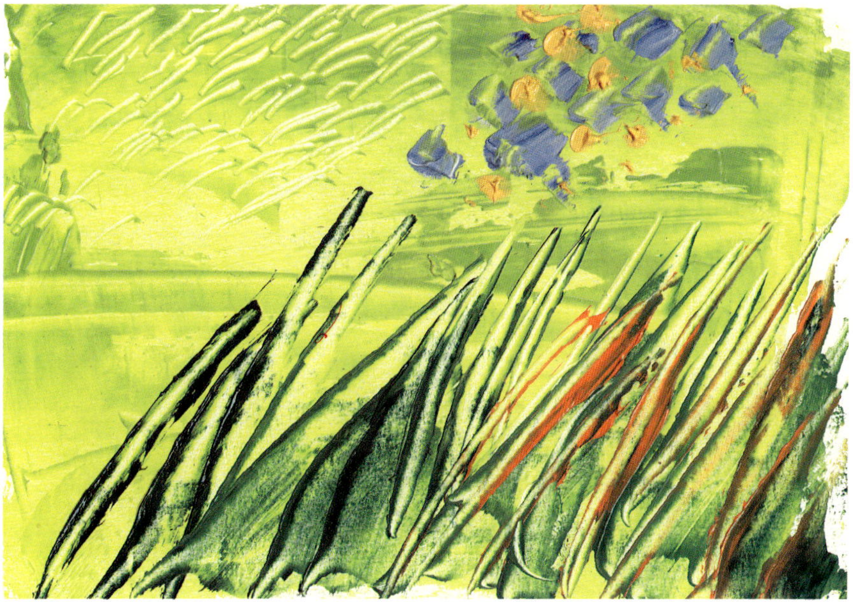

The technique of pressing paper or some other material onto wet paint is called frottage. In the example above, a stiff piece of nonabsorbent tracing paper was pressed onto thin paint and then lifted off again. You can also press differently textured material onto thin coats of paint and then lift it off. The thicker the paint, the more pronounced and three-dimensional the resulting texture.

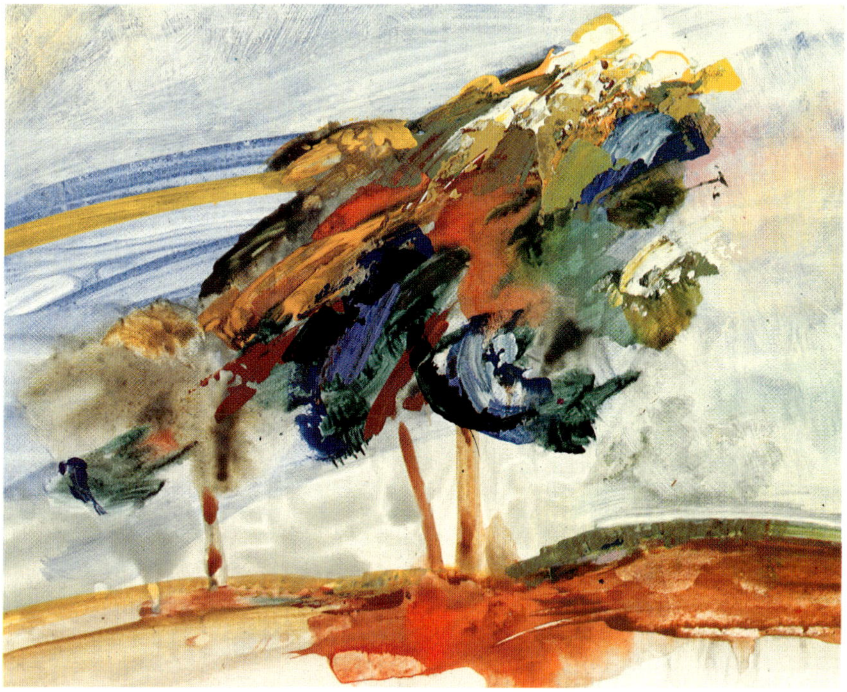

A knife was used to apply the background in the example above. Then lines were scratched in with the handle of a brush, allowing the white background to show through. The dark green was then applied sparingly over the background and scratched into with the handle of a larger brush. A couple thick dots of paint make the composition livelier. This could be a picture of a field of flowers.

The painting to the right shows you that these experiments don't always have to be abstract. Thick paint was applied on top of a glazed background and then worked in various ways. The result is a little painting in which nothing looks realistic, but it is still recognizable as a landscape.

Collages and Wood

Collage can set off your imagination. What would you do with these elements?

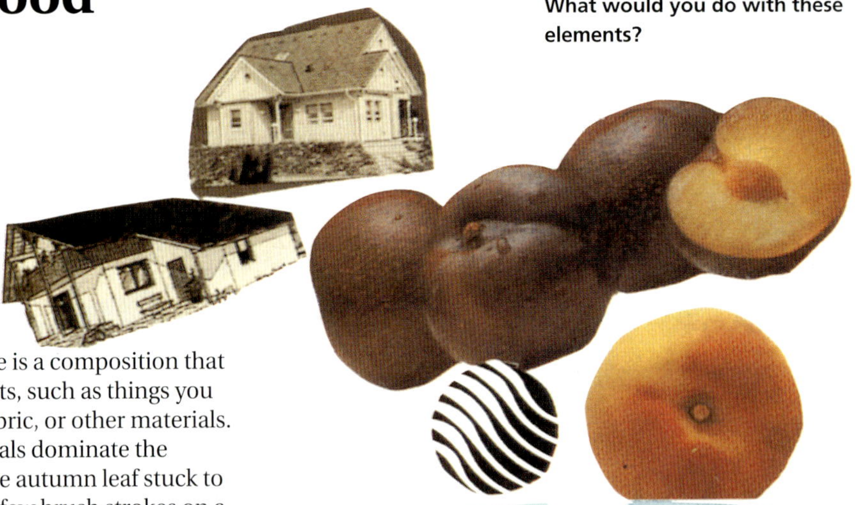

Perhaps you are thinking, "What do collages have to do with oil painting?" Strictly speaking, nothing at all, but if you want to remain open to all the various options and have fun experimenting, you should not overlook this versatile art form. Even if you don't use a collage as a final composition, it can still provide you with inspiration. A collage is a composition that combines painting with other elements, such as things you cut out of the newspaper, scraps of fabric, or other materials. Whether the paint or the other materials dominate the composition is up to the artist. A single autumn leaf stuck to a painting can be just as effective as a few brush strokes on a photo montage.

A few examples: In the picture to the right, the cheese was used as a kind of cliff; in the collage below, photos of unusual items such as hands, vegetables, and a computer were made into a landscape.

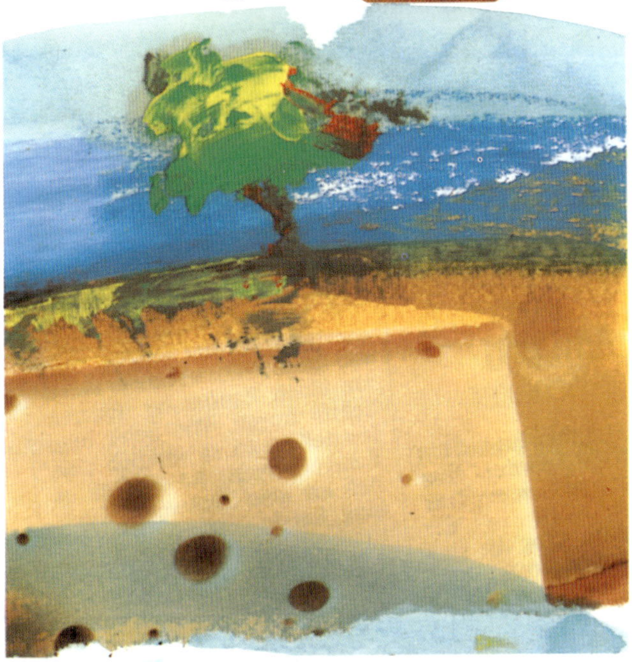

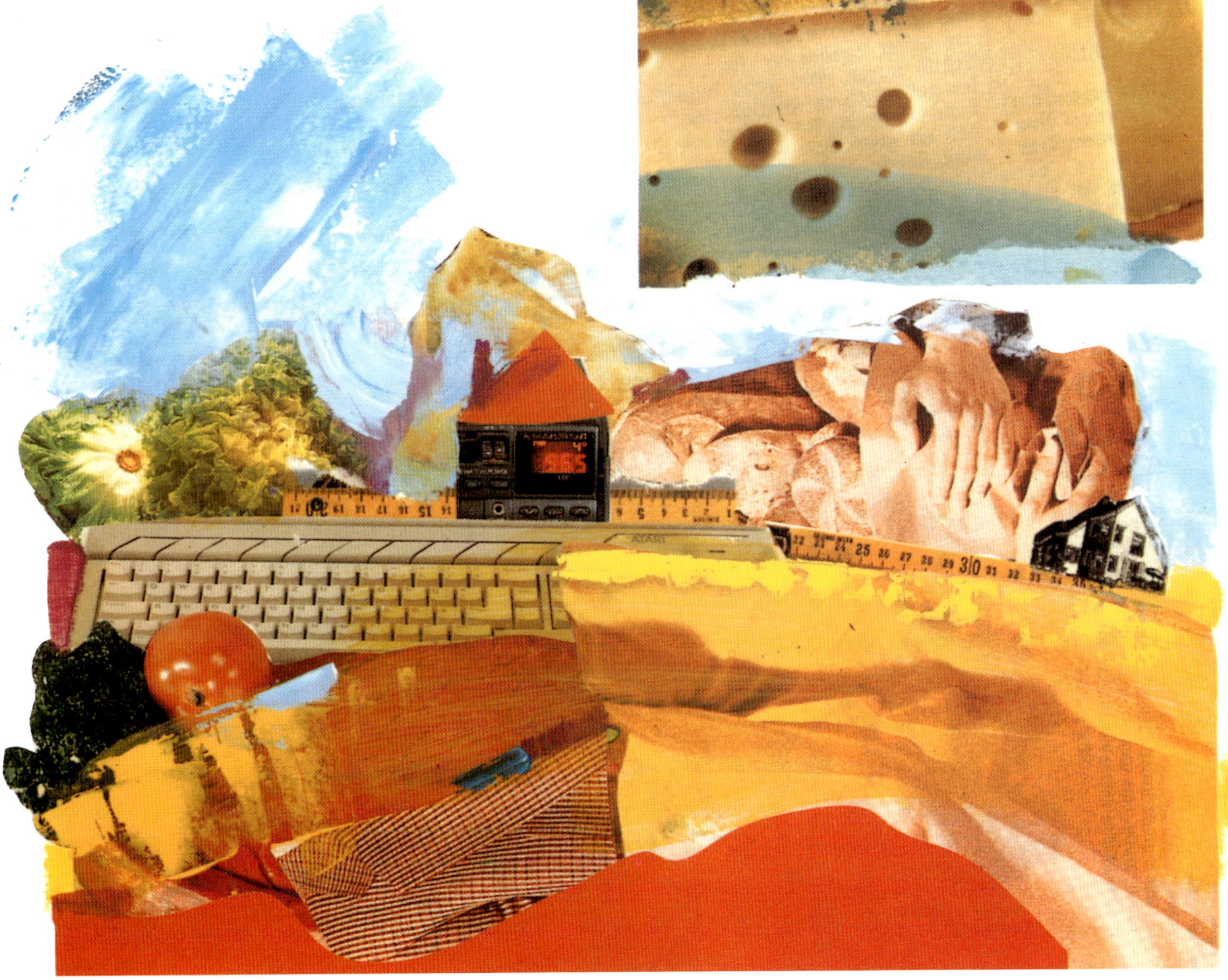

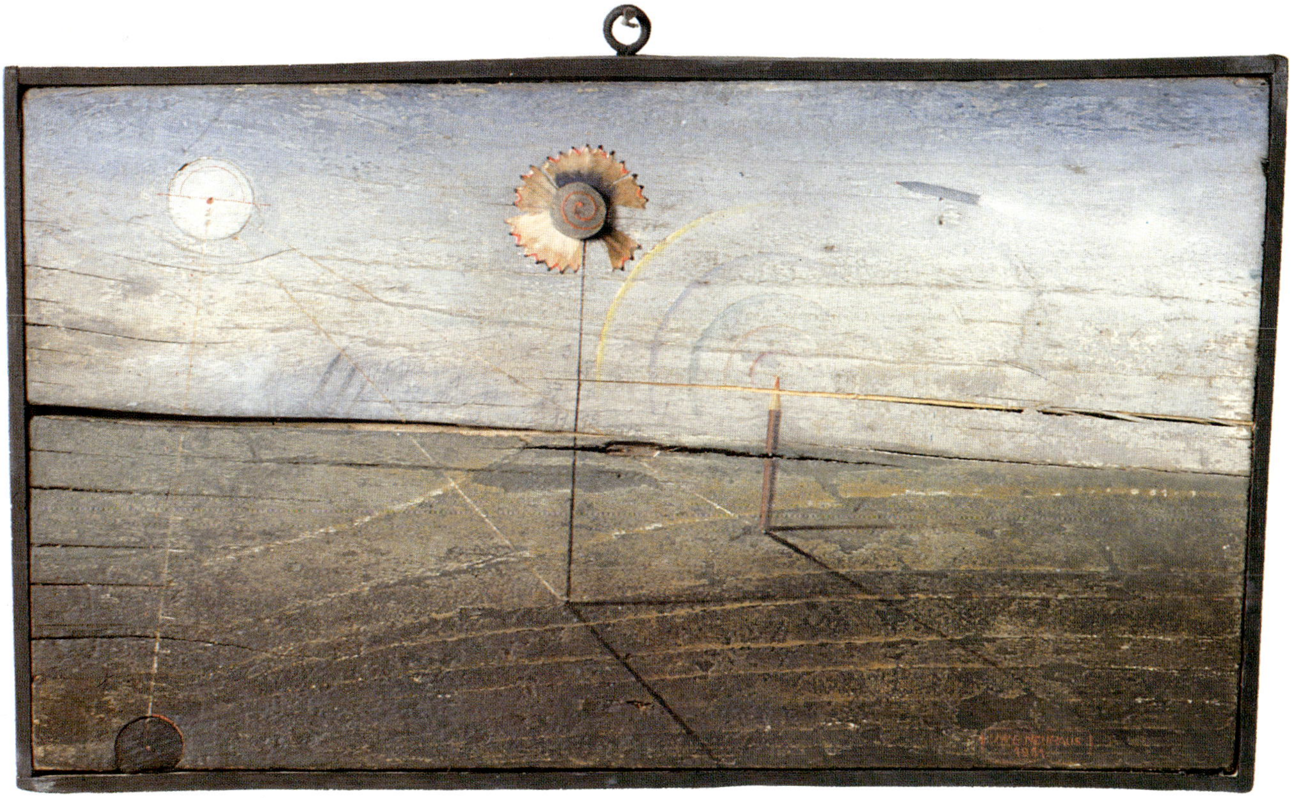

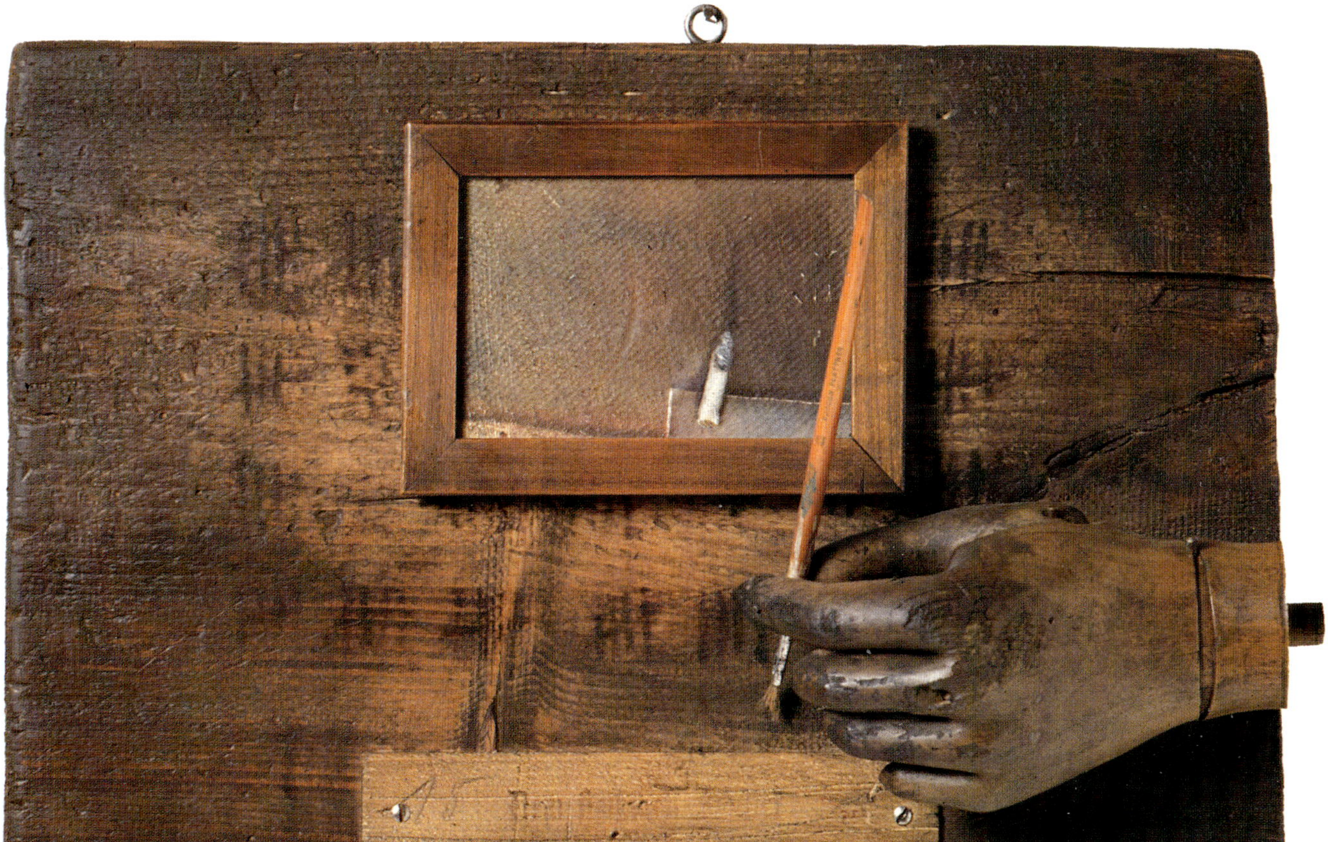

Uwe Neuhaus likes to incorporate the surface or the frame into his paintings. In the uppermost example, he made the grain of the wood into a part of the composition. The grain alone gives the impression of fields, and of distance, which continues off into the sky. This painting belongs to a series entitled "Firewood Pictures."

His composition, *The Diligent Student,* is a different kind of collage. The picture within a picture—the cigarette in the frame—is a highly detailed oil painting. Both the wood in the background and the frame were coated with paint. The hand and the brush were then fastened to it. Sometimes you can find unusual-looking pieces of wood or roots, which you can combine with painting to create interesting compositions.

Motifs for Inspiration

Sometimes you feel like painting, but you don't know what to paint. A sketchpad can help you overcome this block, or you might find interesting motifs in pictures from your last vacation. If you do not have either one or you cannot find anything you like, then maybe one of the motifs below will interest you. Of course, you can make any changes you like; these remarks are merely suggestions.

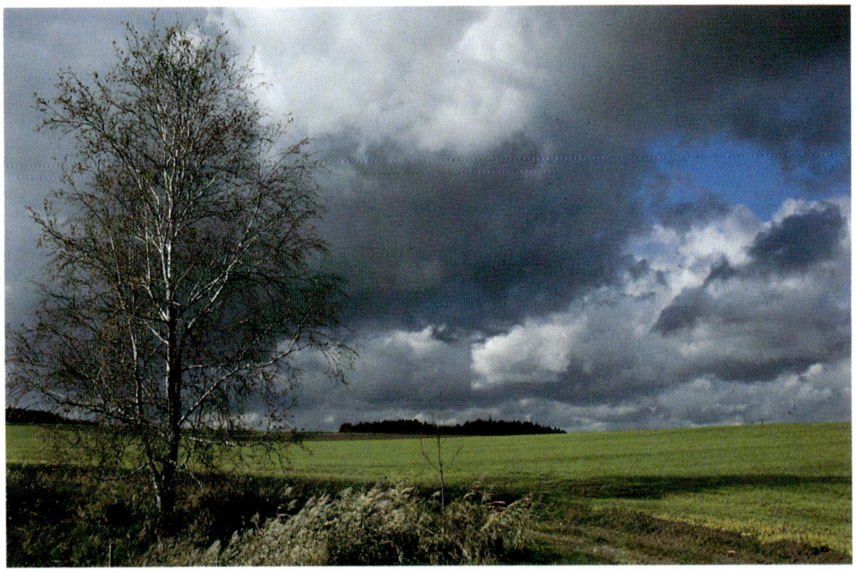

Clouds and stormy skies are always fascinating. Since skies change quickly, it is easier to capture them in a photograph than in a sketch. The examples to the right show two cloud formations. The storm appears to be breaking in the top one. The mood is more dramatic than in the bottom one, where the clouds seem almost friendly. You could use thick coats of paint to mix the gray and white directly on the canvas for the stormy motif. You could use a soft brush to paint the gentle gradation in the landscape for the bottom picture. Use the photo as a model for how clouds look. You can change the composition, perhaps increasing or decreasing the dramatic effect as you like.

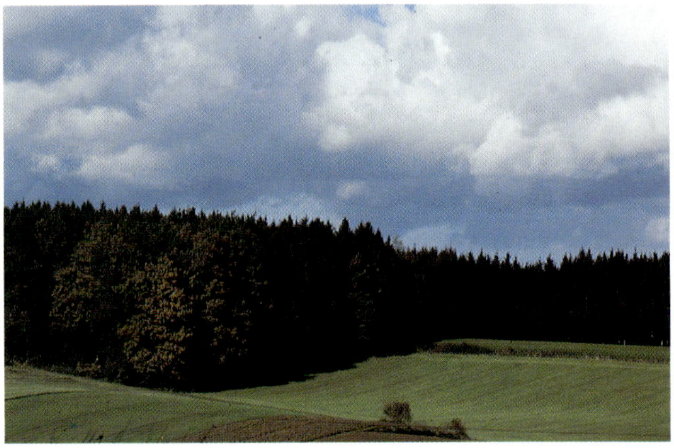

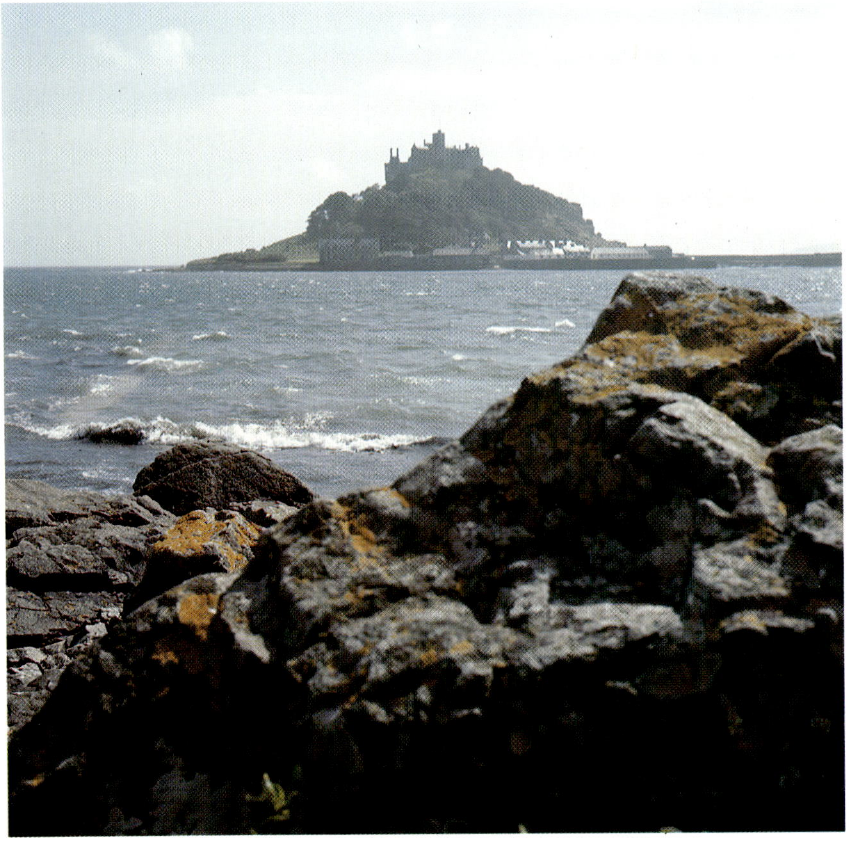

If you like textures, perhaps you would like to try painting the rocks in front of St. Michael, the English counterpart to Mont St. Michel. The moss-covered rocks, with their shadows and abstract shapes, form an interesting contrast to the slight movement in the water and the hazy island. This is an excellent motif for experimenting with textures, brush strokes, and mixtures.

You can change the sizes, perhaps exaggerating the rocks and painting the island in the background. Make a few compositional sketches before you start painting on the canvas.

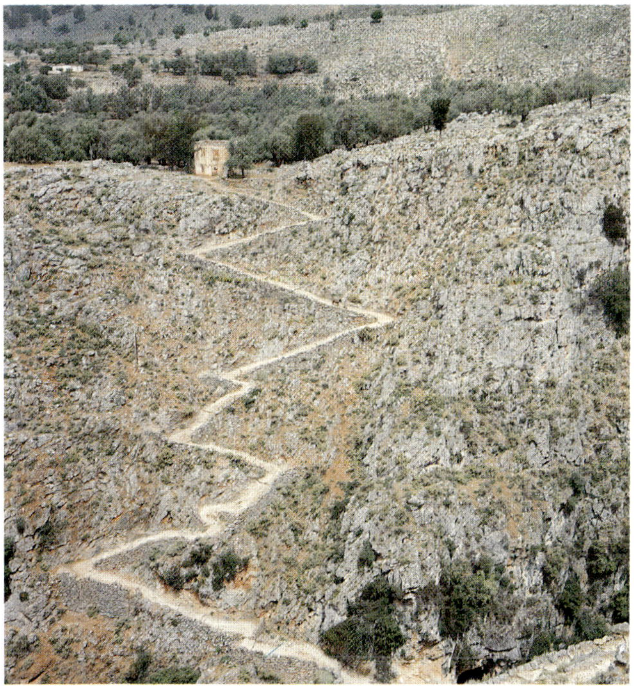

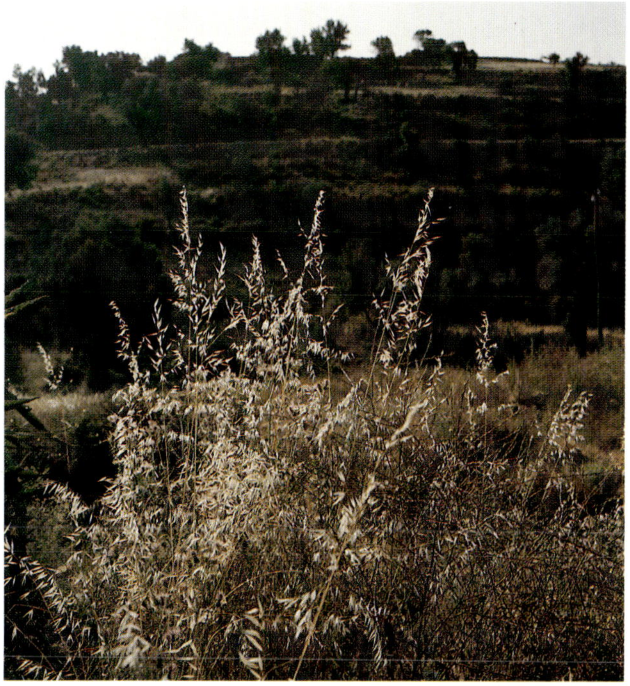

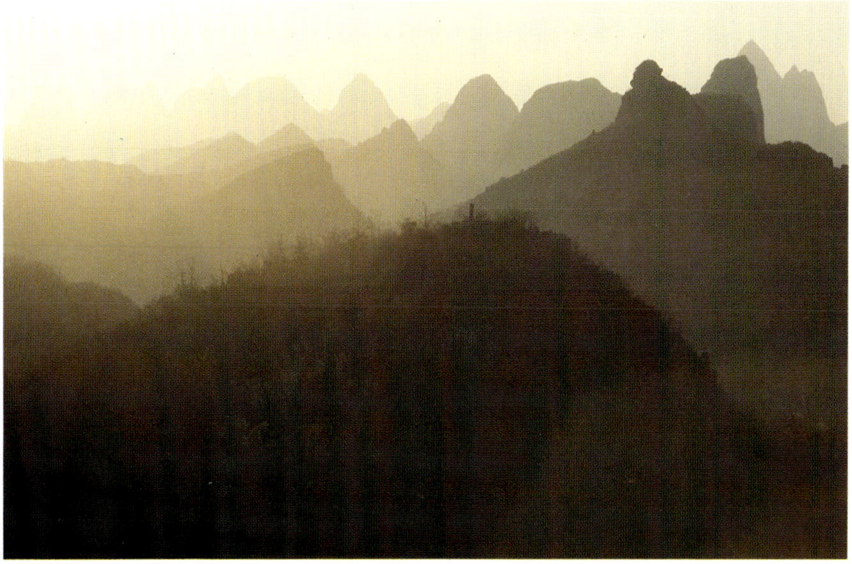

Although they might seem boring at first glance, the two pictures above represent unusual landscape motifs. First, let's look at the bike path on the far left. You could turn the rather monotone mountain into an artistic element, perhaps in the style of pointillism. The bizarre path could be made into a graphical element.

The picture above offers an opportunity for working with layers of paint. The sun-drenched bush could be applied on top of the dark landscape, repeating the highlights throughout the entire picture.

The Chinese landscape shown above is the right choice for fans of gradations and delicate color schemes. The areas that flow into the background, continuously becoming lighter as they go, provide depth and perspective.

The village on the right was built from sun-dried bricks, and your painting should convey this. There is a subtle interplay of textures, shapes, and negative space. You can emphasize the sky and the bushes as you like, reducing them or eliminating them completely.

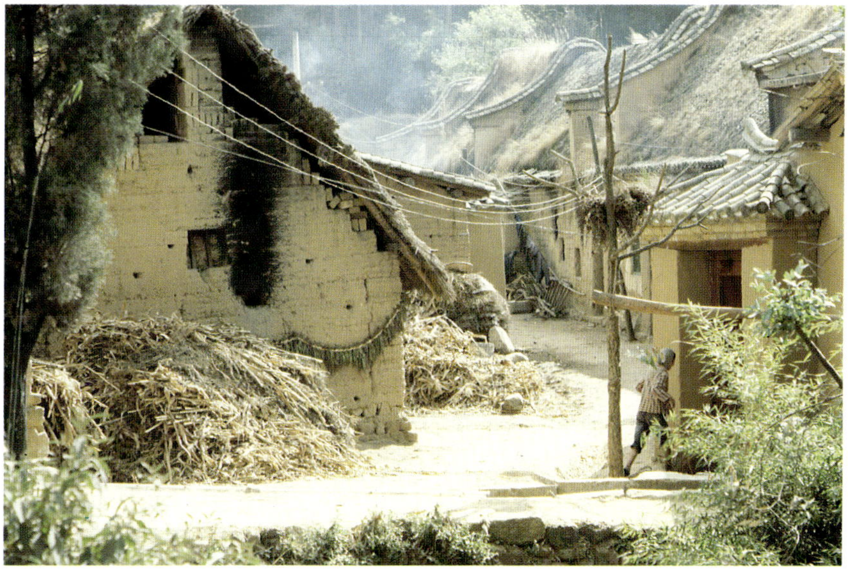

Glossary

cast shadow
The shadow created when an opaque object blocks a light source. The size and shape of the cast shadow are influenced by the position of the light source.

color, darkened
A color that has been mixed with black.

color, lightened
A color that has been mixed with white.

core shadow
The shadow found on an object. The core shadow is nearly always lighter than the cast shadow and gives an object its shape and three-dimensionality.

dry-on-dry
A technique of applying unthinned paint onto a dry base. Depending on the texture of the surface, the artist can achieve interesting effects with this technique.

glaze
A thin, transparent layer of paint applied over dry paint. When applying glazes with oil paints, however, do not apply lean paint (low in oil content) over fat paint (high in oil content). This can result in cracks in the surface of the painting.

gradation
A successive progression of tones, shades, or colors. A gradation can be a transition from dark to light or vice versa. In a gradation from dark to light, increasing amounts of white are added to a hue.

impasto
A thick application of paint. In oil painting, this technique is used to apply thick layers of unthinned or lightly thinned paint with a stiff brush or palette knife so that the paint stands up from the surface, resulting in an obvious texture.

Impressionism
An artistic movement that originated in France in the mid-1860s. The name comes from an 1872 painting by Monet entitled *Impression: Sunrise.* The impressionists were particularly interested in light and color. The artist is led by his visual impressions and attempts to re-create the mood of a subject. The favorite motifs of the Impressionists were animated scenes from daily life and bright landscapes.

movable frame
An adjustable border typically made from cardboard.

negative space
The space that forms between objects in a motif or between the motif and the frame.

oil pastels
A medium made from a mixture of pigment, wax, oil, and animal fat. The resulting paste is molded into sticks. Oil pastels are soluble in turpentine and are water resistant.

one-point perspective
A form of perspective that involves only one vanishing point. If the side of an object is parallel to the picture plane and the line of vision is exactly at its center, the object is said to be in one-point perspective.

plasticity
The effect of three-dimensionality. Just as the sculptor can model a three-dimensional figure, the painter can use techniques to achieve the illusion of space.

positive space
The areas formed by objects in a painting. Positive and negative shapes are always interrelated.

Renaissance
An epoch in art history that can be divided into three periods: the Early Renaissance (ca. 1420), which replaced the Gothic period; the High Renaissance (ca. 1500); and the Late Renaissance (between 1520 and 1530). "Renaissance" is a French word meaning "rebirth" and signifies the revival of Greek and Roman civilization in art and literature. This period is also associated with a break with the church and the feudal order of the Middle Ages. The visual arts reflected these changes, and artists strove for realism in their work. This epoch also witnessed attempts to turn art into a science.

surrealism
A late nineteenth-century and early twentieth-century art movement that uses the psychology of Freud to try to express the workings of the subconscious. The surrealists believed that dreams, drugs, and hypnosis could open the door to the subconscious, which they viewed as the actual reality. Surrealism found its way into the visual arts through the paintings of Giorgio de Chirico and Max Ernst. Other well-known surrealists include Pablo Picasso, Paul Klee, Salvador Dali, Joan Miró, and René Magritte.

tonal value
The degree of darkness or lightness in a color measured on a scale of gradations between black and white.

warm and cool colors
The two basic divisions of the color wheel. The yellows, oranges, and reds are generally regarded as warm colors and the greens, blues, and violets are considered to be cool. In the twelve-color wheel, yellow is the warm pole and purple is the cool pole. The temperature of the colors between them is relative to the colors with which they are contrasted.

wet-in-wet
A technique of working with fresh paint on a wet surface. Working wet-in-wet allows the artist to achieve soft blends and delicate contours.

Credits

Jan van Eyck, *Madonna with Chancellor Rolin* (detail) (page 6): Musée National du Louvre, Paris. Photograph © R.M.N.

Rembrandt Harmensz van Rijn, *Winter Landscape* (page 7): © Staatliche Museen Kassel.

Caspar David Friedrich, *Moonrise Over the Sea* (page 7): ©Staatliche Museen zu Berlin, Preussischer Kulturbesitz, Nationalgalerie.

Vincent van Gogh, *Landscape with Three Trees and a House* (page 26): Collection State Museum Kröller-Müller, Otterlo, The Netherlands.

Edward Hopper, *Corn Hill, Truro, Cape Cod 1930* (page 27): The Mary and Sylvan Collection, McNay Art Museum, San Antonio, Texas.

Claude Monet, *Haystack in the Sunlight* (page 7): Kunsthaus Zürich.

Paul Cézanne, *La Montagne Sainte-Victoire* (page 29): Courtauld Institute Galleries, Courtauld Collection, London.

John Constable, *Willy Lott's House* (page 28): by courtesy of the Board of Trustees of the Victoria & Albert Museum, London.

Titian, *Christ Appearing with the Magdalen* (page 6): reproduced by courtesy of the Trustees, The National Gallery, London.

Photograph on pages 8 and 9 by Ernst Fesseler.

Index

Oils—Landscape
Recommended reading

Foster, Walter T., *Mixing Colors and Materials To Use*. How To Series. Laguna Hills, California: Walter Foster Publishing. 1989. #HT56. ISBN: 1-56010-0546-X.

Palluth, William. *Painting in Oils*. Artist's Library Series. Laguna Hills, California: Walter Foster Publishing. 1984. #AL01. ISBN: 0-929261-01-1.

Powell, William F. *Color (And How To Use It)*. Artist's Library Series. Laguna Hills, California: Walter Foster Publishing. 1984. #AL05. ISBN: 0-929261-05-4.

____________. *Oil Painting Materials (And Their Uses)*. Artist's Library Series. Laguna Hills, California: Walter Foster Publishing. 1984. #AL17. ISBN: 1-56010-056-7.